DATE DUE

JE 22 '93			
NO 24 '93			
MY 27 '94			
DE 9 '94			
MY 17 '96			
JY 21 '98			

DEMCO 38-296

MARKETING TO CHINA

One Billion New Customers

MARKETING TO CHINA

One Billion New Customers

Xu Bai Yi

NTC Business Books
a division of *NTC Publishing Group* • Lincolnwood, Illinois USA

1991 Printing

Contents

Foreword   xi

Preface   xiii

Where Has China Been?   xv

1 Economic Readjustment and Reform
   in China   1
   Managing a Socialist Economy   1
   Shanghai Advances amidst Readjustment   2
   The Sixth Five-Year Plan (1981–1985) and
      the Seventh Five-Year Plan (1986–1990)   3
   People Endorse Reforms   4
   The Open Door Policy   4
   Special Economic Zones   5
   Five Characteristics of Foreign Investments
      in Shanghai   7
   GNP Exceeds One Trillion Yuan in 1987   8
   Some Case Histories   9
   From the Business Pages   11

2 Characteristics of the China Market   17
   Population   17
   Languages   22
   The Traditional Solar Calendar and
      Seasonality   23
   Demographic Trends and Buying Behavior   24
   A Survey of National Character   27
   From the Business Pages   27

3 Applying Western Techniques to Marketing in China — 31
Where Is Your Target Market? — 32
Marketing and Promotional Mix — 33
Advertising Always Pays — 34

4 How to Enter the China Market — 37
China's Import and Export Corporations — 37
China Council for the Promotion of International Trade — 38
Finding the *Hongniang*, or Go-Between — 39
Public Relations and Sales Promotion — 39
Showrooms and Service Centers — 41
Competition Research — 41
From the Business Pages — 44

5 A New Era for Advertising in China — 63
The Major Advertising Companies — 66
Foreign Advertising Agents and Joint-Venture Advertising Agencies — 68
Advertising Associations — 69
China International Exhibition Center (CIEC) — 69
From the Business Pages — 70

6 Advertising Media in China — 71
Newspapers and Advertising Rates — 71
Magazines — 73
Radio and Television — 74
Radio and TV Publications — 76
Outdoor Advertising — 77
Direct Mail — 78
Exhibitions and Mini Sales Exhibitions — 78
Promotions — 79
Media Reach Surveys — 79
From the Business Pages — 83

7 Guidelines for Advertising in China 85
The Local Touch 85
Foreign Label Impact 86
Brand Distinction 87
Some Dos and Don'ts 90
A Fresh Start for Advertising in China 91

Appendixes 93
I. Trademark Law of the People's Republic of China 93
II. Regulations for Advertising Management 103
III. Detailed Rules of Regulations for Advertising Management 109
IV. Provisions of the State Council of the People's Republic of China for the Encouragement of Foreign Investment 119
V. Import and Export Corporations and Enterprises of Various Ministries under the State Council 125

Bibliography and Sources 135

Index 139

List of Tables

Output of Major Industrial Items in 1980   **2**

Selected Industry Targets for 1990   **4**

Ten Cities in the Shanghai Economic Zone and Their
Major Industries   **6**

Retail Sales in 1987   **9**

Population and Area of China's Provinces, Municipalities, and
Autonomous Regions (1982 Census)   **18**

Population of China's Nationalities (1982 Census)   **19**

Families (1982 Census)   **20**

Education Level, per 1,000 (1982 Census)   **21**

Advertising Industry Growth   **63**

Advertising Business Volume, 1986   **64**

Advertising Business Volume by Territory, 1986   **64**

Ten Leading Foreign Advertisers, 1986   **65**

Ten Leading Foreign Advertisers Compared, 1986–1987   **66**

Magazines in China, 1980   **73**

Magazines in Shanghai, 1985   **74**

Advertising Rates, Central TV (U.S. $)   **76**

Advertising Rates, Shanghai TV (U.S. $)   **76**

Audience, by Age (%)   **80**

Audience, by Education (%)   **80**

Interest in Radio Commercials   **80**

Interest in TV Commercials   **81**

Interest in Newspaper Ads   **81**

Advertising Reach, by Vocation (%)   **82**

Foreword

Despite the events in the spring of 1989 that drew world-wide attention, China remains committed to an "open door" policy for foreign investment initiated by then Premier Deng Xiao Ping. Deng stressed China's need for foreign investment to fulfill its economic goals of quadrupling the gross national product and capitalization by the year 2000, and quadrupling the gross national product again in the succeeding thirty years. Given recent events, the need and encouragement for that investment have become even greater.

China is a vast and multifaceted country. Its cultural heritage goes back thousands of years. With a growing population of over one billion people, China remains one of the last great untapped areas of the world for new sales and marketing opportunities. Many leading economists predict that the People's Republic of China will become the world's next great economic power. Any business that desires to participate in a truly global environment cannot afford to ignore these opportunities.

Xu Bai Yi—whose name in Chinese business circles is synonymous with advertising and marketing—has written an invaluable guide for anyone desiring to learn about or participate in the increasingly complex Chinese business community. Marketing to China presents an exciting challenge —one far different from any you may have faced. Of course it requires daring, initiative and capital, the bases of any successful enterprise. And as in any business venture, planning is the key to success. All of this is especially true when doing business in the People's Republic of China.

The Editors
NTC Business Books

Preface

X China is a marvelous country, not only because of its total land area of almost ten million square kilometers, or its population of over one billion people, but also because of its extremely rich cultural heritage. Papermaking, printing, and movable type were invented in China. Advertising can be traced back 5,000 years in Chinese history; it has passed through the many phases of that history, up to, and including the building of socialism.

Under the recent reform, begun by the Chinese Communist Party in 1979, the country has been opened to the outside world; domestic economic policy has been enlivened; and a new page in the history of Chinese advertising has been turned. Many enterprising businesspeople are seeking ways to enter this new Chinese market. Quite a few have already done so with great success.

In February 1986, I wrote a paper entitled, "A Brief History of Advertising in China." As an advertising professional for over half a century, I witnessed the growth of China's advertising industry and spent many years studying the history of Chinese advertising. Many advertising professionals in the United States found my article interesting and said as much to me. Mr. S. William Pattis, President of NTC Publishing Group, while in Shanghai in 1986, encouraged me to write a more detailed account of the subject.

The Introduction to this book furnishes a background of Chinese advertising; it is followed by seven chapters that discuss more recent developments. The appendixes contain a number of legal documents which provide detailed rules and regulations for entering the China market. The book concentrates on the mainland because information and statistics about Taiwan Province are not complete enough at the time of this writing. They may be included in a later edition of this book.

During the course of preparing my manuscript Messers. Harry Briggs, Dan Spinella, Cas Psujek, and Ms. Anne Basye of NTC's editorial staff have been of great help. Hearty thanks to all of them.

This book, finally, may be considered my brainchild, although it is quite basic.

Where Has China Been?

X *Henry Kissinger once said that any foreign policy that excludes a quarter of mankind is doomed to fail. Likewise, any corporation which ignores marketing to a quarter of mankind, although not doomed to failure, is putting its future image and sales in jeopardy.*

LYRIC HUGHES, "Now Is the Time to Enter China," *Advertising Age*, June 9, 1986

X The New Chinese Consumer

Rich Fong couldn't help smiling as he translated his younger cousin's request to the television salesperson on the third floor of Macy's Union Square in San Francisco. Just ninety minutes earlier, Rich had greeted his cousin Chin at the International Terminal of the San Francisco airport. Chin, on a long-awaited visit from his village home in mainland China, told Rich he had come with clear instructions: buy a very special present for Grandmother Fong. Macy's was Chin's second stop in America. The first had been in the nearby Financial District, where Chin had just exchanged his yuan notes for an envelope of crisp American currency.

International retailers have encountered the purchasing power of cousin Chin and the retailers are fascinated. With good reason.

For example, en route to Macy's Chin did not stop to board one of the noisy cable cars that lumbered up Powell Street; nor did he pause on any of the lower floors to gape at the fabulous wealth displayed in the famous American department store. Rich understood Chin's single-mindedness, but he also knew that the array of goods did not overly impress Chin. After all, Shanghai's No. 1 Department Store boasted an inventory equal to several of the largest Woolworth's stores put together. Moreover, Chin's family had ample money in the bank to satisfy their consumer interests. The mission, as Chin already had explained, was not merely to buy a TV for Grandmother Fong, but to buy her the *right* TV. Here in the United States, Chin declared matter-of-factly, you can get exactly what you want.

Rich nodded and looked over the list of twenty-four features (including the multifunction satellite dish control) that Chin wanted to see demonstrated in the set he had requested. Above all, it was clear from the list that for Chin the right TV was a Sony. Despite the salesperson demonstrating four well-priced American-made and Japanese-made models—every one of which had met more than a dozen of Chin's specifications—Chin remained firm on the point of brand. And Sony, Rich knew from the letters and phone calls, had been on the market in China for quite some time, and was well advertised there. Rich knew Chin wouldn't change his mind. It was going to be a long shopping trip.

Increasingly in recent years, international retailers also are appreciating the decision-making process behind Chin's firm desire for a Sony. They understand that his product-line *savoir faire*—as that of the Chinese consumer in general—makes marketing in China a present imperative for western ventures. This loyalty to the identified product, combined with the statistics on the buying power of the Chinese consumers—statistics which are astonishing the demographics experts of the 1980s—leaves only one conclusion: the cumulative wealth and savvy of the Chinese consumer will ripple through the global business network of the 1990s.

Those joint-venturists who already have taken their businesses to China have discovered some unique tendencies in the Chinese consumer. The one specifically illustrated above, the impact of brand-awareness, cannot be overemphasized. The Chinese have an old saying that the entrepreneur would do well to consider: "Whosoever enters first is master." As commercial advertising reemerges in this vast potential market, the older Chinese purchaser remains faithful to the brands he saw in newspapers in the 1930s: Bayer, Klim, Kodak, Camay. But the youth of China remembers only Mao dresses and Party adages. To these people—whose yearly population *growth* alone equals the entire present population of Texas—

anything commercial provides a delightful novelty. A first encounter with a foreign product or service makes a powerful, and lasting, impression.

To make that first impression, you must take advantage of the open door to China, and the time is now. But how do you start a joint venture? What market segment should your business target in China? What are the consumer buying habits? How do the Chinese people characterize themselves? Why does seasonality have such unique impact in China? What are the latest media reach figures? What services does Chinese industry desperately need? Whose attention do you seek in order to attend a trade show or convention?

These are just some of the questions, some of the strategies, explored throughout the following seven chapters of *Marketing to China: One Billion New Customers.* The author has provided page after page of the most current secondary research, as screened through his six decades of personal experience as an advertising professional in China. But before you can apply such contemporary concerns and issues to your own marketing strategies, you first need turn a careful eye to China's past—to the question of where this commercial giant has been.

Any enterprise considering a move into any foreign market must do the necessary homework. With China, the country's history is perhaps more significant than with any other emerging national market. Since spring 1979, the door to China has been opening. Still, it has opened before . . . and there are lessons to be learned from that earlier opening, from the subsequent closing.

Why the Door Was Closed

Around the middle of the Ming Dynasty (1368–1644), China's already centuries-old "natural" economy—consisting of agriculture and the handicraft industry—was first exposed to capitalist means of production with the development of silk and cotton industries in southeastern China. Several thousand textile workshops emerged in the city of Suzhou alone, with each employing large numbers of workers. In these workshops the production was large scale, the division of labor very detailed. The result, in a few industries in this and a few other Chinese cities, was the emergence of a class of workers with nothing to sell save their labor and limited technical skills—an early proletariet.

The rulers of the succeeding Qing government (1644–1911),

however, threw up a resistance to these early capitalist enterprises. The new regime placed limits on the size of handicraft factories and imposed burdensome taxes on merchants. In contrast to the early years of the preceding Ming Dynasty—during which China had actively sought foreign trade and dispatched treasure-filled ships to other parts of Asia and to Africa—the Qing government instituted a closed-door foreign trade policy. Naval strength was reduced and the government discouraged merchants from seeking foreign markets. This renewed spirit of isolationism was perhaps more in line with China's historical desire for self-sufficiency. For the native economy, however, a profound challenge remained: to feed and employ a vast population that had managed to double in size between the eighteenth and nineteenth centuries.

The Qing government, wishing to strengthen its feudal control of the country, maintained its closed door policy. The only port the Qing government kept open for trade was Guangzhou, through which such items as tea, silk, medicine, and porcelain were traded for woolens, cotton textiles, and spices. On the whole, however, the balance of trade was unfavorable for China's trading partners, especially the British. To correct this imbalance, British colonialists began to ship to China huge quantities of opium, which twice led to war because an unyielding Qing government refused to legalize the opium trade.

The port of Shanghai was opened as a condition of the 1842 treaty of Nanjing, which ended the first "Opium War" with Great Britain. The opening of Shanghai and four other ports further accelerated the disintegration of China's feudal economy. Shanghai's ice-free harbor was (and remains) China's finest, with its network of navigable rivers winding deep into the mainland, and within ten years 120 foreign companies had set up headquarters in the port city. An engraving from the period reveals a hive of American and Western European businesses announcing themselves on building fronts across the busy Bund district: Hiram Fogg & Co.; W. R. Adamson & Co.; Wheelock & Co.; Smith, Kennedy & Co.; Turner & Co.; David Sassoon, Sons & Co.; Gibb, Livingston & Co.; Jardine, Matheson & Co.

In 1860, following the second Opium War and a second round of unequal treaties, China's deterioration into semicolonial society was assured. The government was powerless to stop foreign land grabbing, powerless to protect the rights of its citizens. As testimony to the deteriorations in 1868, a sign posted over the entrance to a new municipal park read "No admittance for dogs and Chinese"; the sign was perhaps only more blatantly insulting to the residents of Shanghai than were the thousands of gambling houses, opium dens, and brothels that littered the city.

Meanwhile, foreign capitalists, faced with even fewer restrictions and several additional open ports, turned China into a dumping-ground for their goods and a base for their industrial raw materials. They shipped and sold to China cotton textiles, kerosene, dyes, and sewing needles; the quantity of cotton goods (backed by advertising) increased most quickly. By 1894, more than one hundred foreign-owned factories operated on Chinese soil, with total investment amounting to 28 million yuan.

With China's once independent natural economy now overwhelmed, some of the Qing officials advocated making the country strong and rich by establishing government-backed Western-style factories. In fact, this "Westernization Group" supported despotic rule with a modernized army and navy only insofar as would be useful in suppressing domestic opposition; foreign aggression was not a particular concern of this faction. The "Westernization Group" began to open factories, mines, and transport and communication facilities in order to provide the necessary raw materials and means of transport for their war industries. By 1894, more than twenty such "government-supervised and merchant-managed" enterprises had been established. This embryonic form of bureaucrat-capitalism—absorbing capital from landlords and merchants, but controlled mainly by Qing officials—monopolized production and most definitely hindered the development of national captitalism.

Nevertheless, between 1872 and 1894 hundreds of privately owned enterprises came into operation, with total investment amounting to 6 million yuan and employees numbering around 30,000. Weak compared with both the foreign-owned and the officially managed businesses, these enterprises were characterized by their small size, slender capital (usually less than 100,000 yuan), and a concentration in light industries: silk reeling, cotton textiles, flour milling, paper making, printing, and match manufacturing.

The brief war that broke out with Japan in 1894 further demonstrated the weakness of the Qing government, and the resulting Treaty of Shimonoseki continued the humiliating partitioning of China. A free-for-all followed Japan's victory, with Russia, France, Germany, and Great Britain all scrambling to secure leases, concessions, and various other special privileges. This treatment of China as an all but conquered nation provoked a good deal of internal resentment, which the government hoped would translate into enthusiasm for a reestablished militia. Indeed, one result of this energy was the formation, in some of the eastern provinces, of self-trained militant gangs. Radical elements quickly gained control of the newly organized bands, inciting them to launch numerous attacks on foreigners. When the attacks escalated into the unwieldy national crisis known as the Boxer Uprising, an international military force was sent to China.

Reluctantly, the Qing government now agreed to a series of reforms aimed at hastening Westernization. The educational system was overhauled, with some formerly taboo Western history and ideas introduced into the curriculum. Attempts were made to establish a Western-style representative government. And a flood of foreign goods caused dramatic changes in Chinese lifestyles, affecting each of the four Chinese categories of daily life—*yi* (clothing), *shi* (eating), *zhu* (residing), and *xing* (walking or traveling).

The Chinese began wearing clothes made from imported fabrics and sewn on Singer sewing machines. Bread was introduced, becoming more and more popular as an alternative to the traditional rice, steamed bun, and porridge. Milk became a daily drink of the upper class. The number of brands of coffee on the market, including Maxwell House, Del Monte, and Hills Brothers, attested to the fact that the Chinese were becoming coffee drinkers. The introduction of concrete changed Chinese construction practices forever. Instead of salt, the Chinese began using toothpaste to brush their teeth. Patent medicines provided an alternative to medicinal herbs. Streetcars and baby carts joined the rickshaws on China's teeming city streets.

Naturally, so thoroughgoing a penetration of foreign goods and services was not achieved effortlessly. One hurdle for foreign commodities was their segregation from native products. The character *Yang* affixed to the commodity name readily identified the item as imported. For instance, regardless of the brand name, imported candles were called *Yang Zhu*, imported oil *Yang You*.

A second hurdle—persuading the Chinese to break from tradition—posed no easy task. Cigarettes, for example, were a novelty many Chinese dared not try, even when free samples were given away in the tea houses. Although tobacco had been brought to China in the seventeenth century and its use was widespread, the Chinese clung stubbornly to their pipes. So in addition to the giveaways, representatives of foreign tobacco companies were dispatched to the tea houses, where they would comment to the crowds that invariably gathered around as they smoked, "Ah, good thing, cigarette."

A similar approach was employed by the streetcar companies. First put into operation in Shanghai in 1908, this novel means of transportation initially attracted more curiosity than riders. People crowded into the windows of the tea houses to look at the streetcars, but few rode them for fear of getting an electric shock. Borrowing a technique Chinese peddlers had been using for centuries, the transit companies advertised the safeness of their operations by hiring people to ride the streetcars blowing trumpets and beating drums.

✳ A Golden Age for Advertising in China

In the late nineteenth and early twentieth centuries, most foreign goods gained acceptance through constant advertising in the modern media. These novel vehicles for advertising—mass publications from modern presses, radio broadcasting, electronic displays—arrived in China along with the foreign commodities.

China has had newspapers in some form or another since the eighth century. *Di Bao (Court Gazette)* was an irregularly issued government publication consisting of news of the court and aimed at officials, intellectuals, and rich merchants. Out of a brief experiment allowing the establishment of a publication office run by commoners came *Jing Bao (Peking Gazette)*, but not until 1858 and the publication of *Zhong Wan Sin Pao* was there a Chinese-managed newspaper. Meanwhile, about 200 foreign-owned newspapers and magazines were published in China throughout the nineteenth century, more than sixty in Shanghai alone between 1842 and 1900.

Though introduced by foreigners, Western advertising media and techniques were embraced by the Chinese. Toward the end of the Qing Dynasty, even the government daily *Political Official Gazette* allowed certain organizations—government-run banks, old-style private banks, art display centers, railways, and industrial organizations—to run advertisements. Two of the most successful foreign-owned newspapers in Shanghai, the competing *Shun Pao* and *Sin Wan Pao*, both eventually became Chinese-owned. By 1923, *Sin Wan Pao*, which catered to businessmen as *Shun Pao* catered to intellectuals, had annual advertising revenues of around 1 million yuan. In 1936, *Sin Wan Pao* boasted of a daily circulation of 150,000.

The Chinese publishing giant Commercial Press launched sixteen magazines between 1903 and 1937. Among these, *Eastern Miscellany,* whose circulation reached 50,000 in 1923, and *Women's Magazine* carried the most advertisements, many for American commodities. This increase in American advertisers is partly attributable to Lin Zhen Bin (C. P. Ling), the American-educated "father of Chinese advertising." Upon his return from the United States, Ling went to work for China Publicity Company, a subsidiary of Commercial Press. While there, he managed to solicit a steady run of advertisement requests through a connection (a former classmate) at New York-based National Export Advertising Service.

Another magazine with many advertising pages was *Happy Home,* a women's magazine published between 1935 and 1945. The first issue's 50,000 copies were distributed free of charge. Fifty percent of *Happy Home's* pages were advertising, so the magazine employed the slogan, "A ladies' home journal with direct mail potential, and a guaranteed circulation of 50,000 copies." Beginning with the seventh issue, it was sold through newsstands and subscriptions.

Radio broadcasting in China dates to 1922 and a short-lived fifty-watt American operation. In 1927, the Sun Sun Company, a Shanghai department store, established a station that broadcast market news, current events, and Chinese music. By 1936, Shanghai had thirty-six Chinese-run stations, four foreign-run stations, one station run by the city government, and one run by the Ministry of Communications. Radio was the least-used new advertising medium, but advertisers purchased spots and program time on nearly every station. American-owned Henningsen Produce Company even ran newspaper ads that announced the air times of their radio ads for Hazelwood Ice Cream, boosting sales immediately.

Posters introducing foreign medicines were pasted everywhere, both in urban and rural areas. These were usually brought in from the companies' home countries.

China's first two modern billboards belonged to the British-American Tobacco Company, and were erected in Shanghai—one on the roof of a Nanjing Road tea house and another facing Huangpu Park. Soon countless sites were covered with rows of billboards, many of which advertised American motion pictures.

The first neon sign (for Royal Typewriters) was placed in the window of Evans Book Company on Nanjing Road, Shanghai, in 1926. China's largest neon sign, erected by the American-owned Claude Neon Lights, was the first of two memorable signs to occupy a site opposite Shanghai's Great World amusement center. The sign featured a large clock and an animated sequence in which a Ruby Queen cigarette seemed to jump back into the pack.

On the sides and tops of streetcars, cigarettes, and daily-use articles such as Bovril, a British-made beverage, competed for advertising space with gambling houses.

Many companies also purchased newsletters, leaflets, and other ad mailings. British-American Tobacco Company's monthly *Bei Qing Yan Pao* publicized the capitalist political system in addition to the company's cigarettes. Bayer Pharma Company published a medical journal, *Tien De (God's Virtue) Medical News*, and distributed 100,000 copies of *Family Doctor*, a handbook providing information on common illnesses and available remedies. A free publication offered by another pharmaceutical company contained frequently used English words. Eastman Kodak published *Kodak Photography*.

Much like their Western counterparts, though at a later date, Chinese advertising agencies evolved from space brokers. The first modern agency was C. P. Ling's China Commercial Advertising Agency (CCAA), founded in 1926. The "Big Four"—Ling's agency together with Carl Crow, Inc., Millington Ltd., and Consolidated National Advertising Company—dominated the profession in Shanghai in the 1930s. In "Recording a Decade of Service and Progress: 1926–1936," a booklet issued in commemoration of CCAA's tenth anniversary, Ling reflects upon the tremendous progress made by the Chinese advertising industry:

> Service in advertising was not generally understood at the time we started. "Space brokers" were numerous, soliciting business mostly on rebates. Trained men in copy and art work were hard to find. People were not so advertising-minded as they are today. Despite prejudice and difficulties, we determined to develop a Service based on our intimate knowledge of the market and of the people.
>
> In the early days, ten years back, advertising was not used extensively for sales promotion except by a few foreign importers of patent medicines and cigarettes. The full extent of advertising's economic and social functions was far from being understood and appreciated. Few businessmen would consider an advertising expenditure a sound investment. Many of them were skeptical about this modern method of promoting business. It was difficult to sell them agency service, and this type of service was scarce.
>
> However, from insignificant beginnings, when layouts were incomplete, illustrations crude and appeals weak, advertising has made great strides in China during the past decade. It has advanced in various ways. Today, newspapers, magazines, and trade journals are full of striking advertisements. Posters, show-cards, tin signs, and

painted boards are on display everywhere. Handbills, circulars, leaflets, and other forms of printed matter make frequent visits to the
homes of millions.

China has taken to advertising with a vengeance. Every business,
big or small, has come to recognize this vital force. Every manufacturer is keen to draw up an annual budget for this purpose. More
technical men in the field are being trained by national advertisers
and reputable agencies.

Of course, China still has far to travel in this enormous field
before reaching the standard attained by many Western nations.
But, with the growing interest on the part of both advertisers and
consumers and with the changing conditions in this great country,
socially, industrially and economically, the future holds . . . un-
bounded prospects.

Chinese advertising's golden age more or less coincided with an
era now known in China as the Second Revolutionary Civil War
(1927–1937). Actually, these were comparatively quiet years, following as they did a period of nearly constant civil strife that had
troubled China since 1921.

In 1919, the Kuomintang (Nationalist) party had been swept into
office on the wave of fierce patriotism that followed student-led
protest (the May Fourth Movement) over provisions in the Treaty
of Versailles, and aspects of feudalism and imperialism (especially
the restoration of Japanese "privileges" in Shandong province)
which continued after the war. The Communists, meanwhile, had
benefited from an extraordinary increase in the number of industrial workers in China—up from around a half million when the
Bourgeois Revolution toppled the Qing government in 1911 to two
million in 1919. During China's First Revolutionary Civil War
(1921–1927), both the Nationalists and the Communists agreed on
a policy of strikes and boycotts that ultimately led to the disposses-
sion by force of the propertied class and foreigners.

However, a rift developed within the Kuomintang over the direc-
tion and extent of future reforms, leading, by 1927, to a purge of
leftists and Communists by Chiang Kai-shek and the party's moder-
ate and right-wing factions. Subsequently, the Kuomintang party
achieved a degree of stability by instituting various internal reforms and establishing more equal relations with foreign powers.
Far from being eliminated, however, the Communist threat intensi-
fied during this period with the establishment of a People's Army
and the Rural Revolutionary Bases.

During World War II and the Japanese aggression, the Nationalists and Communists once again put aside their differences in a

spirit of cooperation. But with the defeat of their common enemy in 1945 came an immediate renewal of internal hostilities. After some initial success in recapturing areas previously "liberated" by Communist forces, the Nationalists found themselves overextended militarily. More damaging still was the erosion of the party's popular support, due in large measure to the inflation-ravaged economy. In less than four years, the Nationalists were pushed off the mainland entirely. And on October 1, 1949, 300,000 citizens gathered on the Tiananmen Square, Beijing, to attend the ceremony that marked the formal beginning of a new nation, the People's Republic of China.

The next three years China's government devoted to rebuilding the war-torn national economy. The immediate goals were summed up on a banner outside the East China Native Products Exposition in Shanghai in 1951: "Mutual Aid between Town and Country, Promote the Interflow of Commodities, Increase Production, and Make the Economy Prosper." The government's extensive use of billboards and neon signs in a similar exposition in Shanghai later that same year gave some encouragement to the advertising industry, which had been waiting to see what place, if any, it would have in post-Liberation China. But a greatly diminished role for advertising was a foregone conclusion given the Communists' plans to impose strict control on production, consumption, and prices—and of course given their ideological aversion to advertising as a tool of capitalism.

Shortly thereafter, the government set a deadline of January 1956 for the transformation of private businesses to "whole people enterprises." Bureaucrat-capitalist industries were simply expropriated by the state, while a policy of utilization, restriction, and transformation was instituted for purely capitalist industry. Private owners were bought out. Shanghai's 108 advertising agencies had to amalgamate under the identity of the Shanghai Advertising Corporation.

The period of relative stability and order that followed this full-scale socialist reconstruction was in turn followed by an eleven-year period of inexplicable chaos. Beginning in 1966, people in positions of authority—government officials, teachers, factory managers—fell prey to seemingly random acts of persecution. Consequently, an eerie sameness, adopted by many as a survival tactic, settled in: everyone dressed alike; displays of frivolity of any sort were frowned upon; shop windows and billboards were pasted over with red paper and political slogans; neon signs were knocked down.

Over a decade later, in 1976, the overthrow of the counterrevolutionary clique signalled the beginning of a new historical period in China. The reinstatement of former high-ranking government officials immediately and effectively discredited the foregoing Cultural Revolution. Out of the new government's decision to shift the focus of the party's work to socialist modernization in line with the policy of "emancipating the mind, using the brain, seeking truth from facts, and unity to look forward," emerged the political and economic climate that exists in China today.

✗ Whosoever Enters First
Is Master

An official of the Qing government (1644–1911) once mused, "If the Chinese decided this afternoon to add one inch to the sleeves of their jackets, all the factories of Lancashire could not meet the demand in a thousand afternoons."

The current Lever Brothers United Kingdom's joint venture with Shanghai Soap, for example, will put two billion bars of Lux Beauty Soap on the Chinese domestic market in 1989. As you'll read in this book, the Lux label had been seen before in China, but not since Liberation. In that earlier time, the brand name had become synonymous with the product; shoppers bought "Lux," not "facial soap." Upon its current return to the shelves under the joint venture agreement, and with the carryover of earlier brand awareness, first-year volume for Lux was limited not by demand but by the existing output capabilities of Shanghai Soap's plants.

There were times before when the market in China presented to the rest of the world a magnificent opportunity for doing business. Once, long ago, the equivalent of today's entrepreneur depended on heroic seamanship and accurate mariner's maps to recover a splendid bounty of gold and goodwill. Today, the potential rewards—for Lux, for Sony, for your enterprise—are equally great. This time the navigation is only as tricky as choosing your long-distance phone carrier. Why wait?

1

Economic Readjustment and Reform in China

✕ Managing a Socialist Economy

In 1978, the Chinese Communist Party Central Committee decided to spend several more years on further readjustment of the economy. This policy has enabled China's national economy to remove the obstacles to healthy economic development.

One of the aims of current economic readjustment has been to balance the branches of the economy, limiting heavy industry so that the process of production, distribution, circulation, and consumption can be speeded up. To realize this change, the production of consumer goods will be given an important position.

Since 1978, agriculture has advanced and record harvests have been reaped. Priority has been given to the development of light industry, whose rate of growth has greatly surpassed that of heavy industry.

Greater attention is attached to absorbing foreign production techniques suitable to China's national condition. China will use foreign funds and introduce advanced technology from other countries. With its rich resources and huge potentialities, China is a promising market. Economic cooperation between China and other countries has, therefore, a bright future.

1

Before the reforms, capital goods (production) were not considered commodities, with the result that they were all allocated according to state plan and could not circulate on the market. This greatly restricted the scope of commodity circulation. Consumer goods (subsistence) were deemed commodities, but the State commercial departments' rigid control of them caused serious dislocations between production and marketing. Since 1979, therefore, the emphasis has been on creating smooth circulation channels.

Overall, current economic policies seek the extension of the enterprises' right of self-management, regulation by market under the guidance of state planning, and the combination of necessary economic mechanisms with administrative intervention. All this is an experiment in better management of the socialist economy.

Shanghai Advances amidst Readjustment

Shanghai is China's biggest industrial city, and as such plays a vital role in the nation's economy. It is also one of China's oldest cities, with a century and a half of development behind it. Since Liberation in 1949, Shanghai has built up a comprehensive industrial base with effective management and a high level of specialization.

In 1980, while Shanghai's industrial fixed assets accounted for only one-twentieth of the national total, its industrial output value constituted one-eighth of the national total; value of exports one-seventh; and revenue one-sixth. Per-capita income amounted to 2,486 yuan (about U.S. $670), six times the national average.

Output of Major Industrial Items in 1980

Product	1980 output (millions)	Compared with 1949 (% increase)
Steel (tons)	5.21	100,100
Steel products (tons)	4.13	27,400
Metal-cutting machines	.016	2,350
Cotton yarn (bales)	2.12	300
Cotton cloth (meters)	1,614.00	250
Sewing machines	2.26	50,100
Bicycles	3.76	85,400

Source: *China Today*, Series No. 3, 1982.

and border areas, cities and countryside, and between all trades and enterprises.

Besides the four special economic zones (see the following section), China has fourteen coastal cities: Tianjin, Qinghuangdao, Dalian, Yantai, Qingdao, Lianyungang, Nantong, Shanghai, Ningbo, Wenzhou, Fuzhou, Guangzhou, Zhanjiang, and Beihai. As of January 1989, 145 municipalities and counties were included in the list of open cities, bringing the total to 571.

Special Economic Zones

China's special economic zones, the pioneers in the State's economic reforms, are making new efforts to improve production and boost business.

An approved project in the Shenzhen Special Economic Zone is to build an extensive oil refinery with investment by a company from the United Arab Emirates. Construction is expected to start in 1988.

From 1979 to 1986, the Shenzhen Special Economic Zone signed contracts with twenty-one countries and areas in the world—a total contract investment of U.S. $3.974 billion. Of this, $3.109 billion was from Hong Kong, $247 million from Japan, $138.6 million from the United States, and $479 million from other countries and areas.

Elsewhere, in Tianjin Economic and Technical Development Area, 215 contracts have been signed for a total of U.S. $521.97 million, of which foreign capital accounts for $239.36 million (figures from *China Daily*, November 15, 1987).

In 1987, fifty of those already in operation had a combined output value of $170 million and profits of $9.5 million (figures from *China Daily*, January 22, 1988).

Shanghai has developed two economic and technological zones in the past few years. One is the Hongqiao New Area and another is Minhang Economic and Technological Development Zone. Minhang, a small economic zone which covers only 2.13 square kilometers, has already attracted some twenty foreign investors to open businesses in the past few years, including W. R. Grace and Company of the United States (figures from *China Daily*, November 15, 1987).

Ten Cities in the Shanghai Economic Zone and Their Major Industries*

City	Product
Shanghai	airplane, automobile manufacture, shipbuilding, computers
Jiangsu Province:	
Nantong	harbor industry, spun cotton
Changzhou	hand cultivators, transformers
Wuxi	integrated circuits, diesel engines
Suzhou	silk and satin, refrigerators
Zhejiang Province:	
Jiaxing	spun wool, processed foods
Shaoxing	wine, small electric appliances
Ningbo	optics, harbor industry
Huzhou	silk and satin, industrial electronics
Hangzhou	silk and satin, audio electronics

*Up to January 1989 the following cities are included: Xuzhow of Jiangsu Province; Hefei, Bangbu, of Anhui Province; Nanchang, Jiujiang, of Jiangxi Province; and Fuzhou, Xiamen, of Fujian Province.

A third economic zone known as Shanghai Caohejing Hi-Tech Park was set up in July 1988.

Both foreign and domestic businesspeople can set up ventures in the fields of biotechnology, microelectronics, information technology, optic fiber telecommunications, lasers, aeronautical technology, precision instruments, and electronics in the 5-square-kilometer zone.

Two joint ventures have been set up there, the Sino-U.S. Foxboro Co., Ltd., one of the ten best joint ventures in China, and a Sino-Canadian printing circuit venture (*China Daily*, July 25, 1988).

The special economic zone of Xiamen will have 230 foreign-funded enterprises by the end of 1988. Mayor Zou Erjun promised to continue helping investors improve investment conditions.

In the new year, Zou Erjun said, Xiamen will boost both its processing with supplied materials, and assembling with supplied parts and compensation trade, and contract out the retooling of 170 existing enterprises. He welcomed foreign investment in these projects, which are mainly in the textile, garment, light industry, food processing, electronics, and machine building industries (figures from *China Daily*, January 9, 1988).

Retail Sales in 1987

	1987 (billions of yuan)	% increase over 1986
Food	276.3	18.1
Clothing	88.0	13.9
Consumer goods	147.2	16.7

Source: *China Daily*, January 7, 1988.

In Shanghai, GNP in 1987 reached 500 billion yuan, an 8 percent increase over 1986. Industrial-agricultural output value increased 6 percent over 1986. Export reached U.S. $4 billion, a 10 percent increase over 1986 (figures from *Shanghai Statistical Yearbook 1988*, pp. 18, 101).

Some Case Histories

Beijing Jeep

Beijing Jeep Corporation, a joint venture between Beijing Automotive Works (68.6 percent) and American Motors Corporation (31.4 percent) saw its fourth year of operation in 1987. In 1986, Beijing Jeep Corporation produced a record 23,972 four-wheel-drive vehicles.

Since its September 1985 introduction into the Chinese market, Jeep Cherokee has been very successful. Beijing Jeep Corporation is now exporting the Cherokee to customers in Asia and Central America.

The joint venture has annual sales of more than 400 million yuan, and since it went into operation, has earned 130 million yuan in profit.

Shanghai Volkswagen

A Sino-West Germany joint venture, Shanghai Volkswagen has been operating since 1985. Fifteen thousand vehicles were produced in 1988. A goal of 20,000 vehicles has been set for the year 1989. Most of the parts will be produced domestically (currently, 30.6 percent of the Santana's parts are Chinese).

To introduce the new Shanghai Santana model, newspaper, billboard, and transit advertising were used. (In its English advertisement, the headline reads, *German Technology Built in Shanghai for China.*)

The annual appropriation for advertising is said to be around one million yuan. The Santana has quickly become a successful seller in China.

In addition, Guangzhou Peugeot and Tianjin Daihatsu are also producing vehicles and advertising.

Judging by the automobile industry's capability and the goal set in the Seventh Five-Year Plan, the annual vehicle output is expected to reach 600,000 in 1990, with an average yearly increase of 8.5 percent.

Emphasis will be on heavy-duty trucks and light vehicles, paving the way for the development of car production, according to Chen Zutao, General Manager of the China Automobile Industry Corporation (from "Auto Industry Picking up Speed," *China Daily,* June 23, 1987).

Joint venture motor enterprises are rolling fast on China's roads and foreign producers want to invest in the industry.

Dong Yiru, an official from the China National Automotive Industry Corp., said that six new joint ventures have opened in the country, pushing the number of motor industry ventures to thirteen, with a foreign investment of U.S. $150 million (*China Daily,* January 15, 1989).

Sino-American Shanghai Squibb Pharmaceuticals, Ltd.

Squibb was a famous brand name before Liberation. Among its many products, Calcium Panthothenate Tablet advertised extensively in newspapers. Now it is produced as part of a Sino-U.S. joint venture in Shanghai. (A modern multiproduct plant has been built and is run strictly in accordance with the U.S. Food and Drug Administration's "good manufacturing standards" [GMP].) Production started in October 1985 without advertising and initial sales were not very encouraging. From July 1986, advertising in newspapers started with an appropriation of approximately 140,000 yuan for that purpose. Sales increased in August and September and rose sharply in November. Now fifteen medicines are on sale in sixty-three cities. The total sales volume of 1986 was 13 million yuan; in 1987, the volume reached 27 million yuan. A 40 percent increase is expected in 1988. The venture is making money.

Theragran-M is well received, for example, because the retail price of 8 yuan for thirty daily tablets seems reasonable to customers.

The success of Squibb is due also to the close cooperation of Chinese and American staffs; the head office sent fifty groups of experts to supervise the production. It has proven to be one of the most successful of the forty overseas companies linked with Squibb.

China-Schindler Elevator Company, Ltd.

Established in 1980, one of the first joint ventures in the industrial sector of China was jointly operated by China Construction Machinery Corporation, Swiss Schindler Holdings AG, and Jardine Schindler (Far East) Holdings SA of Hong Kong. The joint venture operates two elevator factories, one in Shanghai and the other in Beijing. A third is planned for Suzhou, Jiangsu Province. The company produces lifts and escalators and about 30 percent of its output is exported.

In its first year, CSE manufactured U.S. $345,000 worth of equipment. In 1986, the amount jumped to $8.15 million. The company has produced 6,600 lifts, representing an average increase of about 28 percent annually. It has earned $25 million in profits over the past seven years.

From the Business Pages

A sampling of newsclips from *China Daily* suggests the magnitude and diversity of outside investment in China.

"Hot Spots" for Outside Investment

The suburban areas of Shanghai, China's largest industrial and commercial city, are becoming "hot spots" for foreign investment. Fifty-six internationally invested ventures are operating in the ten suburban counties with a total direct investment of $130 million. Most of these ventures are involved in light and textile industries as well as arts and crafts and agricultural animal husbandry.

Shanghai Xin Yi Wooltex Corporation, a joint venture in Songjiang County, set a record in the city by recovering its initial investment in a little over thirteen months.

One of China's largest joint ventures in agriculture and animal husbandry, Shanghai Da Jiang Co., Ltd., has established a large automated plant to raise chickens, and after one year of operation its products are already exported abroad. The Thai side of the venture said such rapid development was beyond their expectations (January 23, 1988).

Giant Coal Mine Shows Sino-Foreign Cooperation

Work continues in the operation of a $650 million joint venture at Antaibao in Shanxi Province, one of the largest open-cast coal mines in the world (September 11, 1987).

China, U.S. Sign a Large Auto Deal

The First Automobile Works of Changchun, a giant Chinese auto manufacturer, signed an agreement in Beijing with Chrysler Motors Corporation of the United States to buy machinery and technical help for a new factory to produce up to 300,000 engines a year for light trucks and cars (July 22, 1987).

Australia Invests in Aluminum

China and Australia signed their largest joint venture agreement, heralding a new era in China's fast developing aluminum industry (June 30, 1987).

Gateway to China's Canadian Trade

Canadian Consul General Christian Sarrazin said during an interview, "We Canadians feel there's more potential in trade in Shanghai. The business community in Canada has great interest in your city" (July 25, 1987).

Medicine Firms Find the Right Formula

There are five pharmaceutical joint ventures in China. They include the China Otsuka Pharmaceutical Co., Ltd. (with Japan), the Sino-Sweden Pharmaceutical Co., Ltd., the Sino-American Suzhou Capsugel Ltd. and Shanghai Squibb Pharmaceuticals Ltd., and Janssen Pharmaceuticals Ltd. (with Belgium). More than 20 are in the course of negotiation (July 14, 1987).

The Chinese policy attracted many countries to invest in. Saeed Jumma Al Naboodah, head of a delegation from Dubai, is negotiating to invest tens of millions (U.S. $) in China's light and chemical industries. He said in an interview with *China Daily*, "After talking with Chinese government leaders, I got to know China's determination to carry out its open policy. The operation of foreign-backed ventures has also showed China's ability to manage joint ventures" (June 27, 1987).

Philadelphia-based Pharmaceutical Company Starts China Venture

The U.S. $3.5 million venture between Smithkline Beckman and Tianjin Branch of China National Medicinal Corporation and Tianjin Hebei Pharmaceutical Co. is the second Sino-American pharmaceutical manufacturing plant.

By the end of 1988, the Tianjin plant will be able to produce five of Smithkline's pharmaceutical products using original trademarks like Zental, Tagamet, and Contac (November 1, 1987).

Large Glass Plant Goes into Production

A Sino-British joint venture, the Shanghai Yaohua Pilkington Glass Corporation, can produce 200,000 tons of float glass annually with a thickness of between 2–25 mm. Some will be exported. The plant, representing an investment of 432 million yuan (£70.5 million), is among the largest Sino-foreign joint ventures (January 3, 1988).

Czech Machinery Makes New Shoes

A shoemaking production line, operating on 18 essential machines received from Czechoslovakia through barter trade, went into production in December 1987. The new line is expected to produce 255,000 pairs of leather shoes every year, earning an output value of 3.44 million yuan.

The total value of the production line was 2.49 million yuan including the 580,000 Swiss francs worth of Czechoslovakian machinery.

Josef Cilek, commercial attache of the country's embassy in Beijing, said barter between the two countries has developed quickly in the past few years. An exhibition of Czechoslovakian machinery is to be opened in Shanghai on July 15, 1988 (December 31, 1987).

Japanese Giant Seeks Cooperation

The Matsushita Electric Industrial Co., of Japan, maker of National and Panasonic brand products, is changing its business policy in China. Instead of mainly selling goods, it will seek to establish cooperative efforts, including joint ventures and coproductions.

The Beijing Matsushita Color Cathode Ray Tube Co. — the first joint venture between Matsushita and China with a total investment of 20 billion Japanese yen (about U.S. $140 million) — aims to provide the domestic market with high-quality TV tubes as well as exporting some to keep a foreign exchange balance (October 18, 1987).

Lufthansa to Invest in Maintenance Center

A 600-million-yuan aircraft maintenance center in Beijing — a 50/50 joint venture between the Civil Aviation Administration of China and Lufthansa Airlines — was approved by the State Council in 1987. When the center is completed in about two or three years, it will be able to repair all types of Boeing airplanes as well as airbuses and other aircraft (October 18, 1987).

Johnson Wax in Joint Venture

Sino-American Johnson Ltd., an equity joint venture partnership formed by Johnson Wax of the United States and the Shanghai Consumer Chemical Industrial Development Corporation, was formed in 1987.

With an investment of $7.2 million from Johnson Wax, the joint venture is the 45th enterprise in the country's largest city involving American investment.

Initially, Johnson Ltd. is marketing health care and shoe care chemical specialty products. For the first year of the joint venture, the annual sales value is projected to be 90 million yuan.

Shanghai Johnson is the 47th overseas subsidiary in 44 countries of the 101-year-old Johnson Wax Co., which sold its wax in China before the Liberation. Now Johnson Ltd. is advertising on a billboard on Huai-hai Road, Shanghai for Sea-gull Hair Care and Red Bird Shoe Care — two existing brands. An expanded line of products using Johnson Wax technology will be introduced [In the latter part of 1988, a new shampoo, Agree, was marketed with teaser advertising in newspapers, on billboards, and on the side panels of buses.] (November 15, 1987).

Joint Venture Planned to Expansion

The Shanghai Wang Computer Development Co. — a Sino-American joint venture set up in October 1986 — is satisfied with its year-long cooperation and is implementing its expansion plan.

Optimistic about the future, the two sides will make a total additional investment of U.S. $900,000, of which Wang Laboratories of the United States will inject 60 percent and the Shanghai Computer Development Co. the remainder.

The venture has sold the 40 VS small computers and 300 CCS work stations it has produced — a sales volume of about $3.5 million, and 24 million yuan.

The joint venture advertised in the English *China Daily*, as well as Chinese newspapers (October 25, 1987).

Parasite-killing Chemical Plant

Shanghai No. 2 Pharmaceutical Factory signed a contract with Essix Asia Ltd. under the Schering Corporation of the United States for joint production of a kind of high-tech parasite-killing chemical.

William Outch, director of the Schering's technical service, Asia-Pacific region, said, "Shanghai No. 2 Pharmaceutical Factory is the most suitable partner in Asia, as it is strong in technical expertise, sound in management and reliable in quality of products."

According to the contract, Schering will provide all the technology for the production of the chemical, Netobimin. The annual output will be 30 tons (December 12, 1987).

GM to Aid China's Automotive Industry

The China National Automotive Industry Corporation and General Motors of the United States announced a multiphase umbrella agreement in Beijing.

Under the agreement, GM will cooperate with a number of Chinese motor vehicle production enterprises in order to assist the development of China's automobile industry.

Barton Brown, president of GM Overseas Corporation, said the long-term umbrella plan between GM and China, when fully implemented, will reflect the broadest involvement in China's auto industry by any foreign corporation (January 22, 1988).

Products for Export

The Beijing Philips Audio/Video Corporation, the capital's first electronics joint venture, has put its product onto the international markets. In early August 1987, 23,000 recorders were exported to Austria, Spain, Holland, Venezuela, Malaysia, the Philippines, and elsewhere. They earned U.S. $300,000.

With a total investment of $4.8 million, the Beijing Philips Audio/Video Corporation went into operation in July 1987. It is one of the four audio/video corporations jointly controlled by Holland Philips Transnational Corporation in Asia (October 30, 1987).

China, U.S. to Join in Producing Cigarettes

American and Chinese cigarette producers came together in October 1988 for the inauguration of the first joint-venture cigarette factory in China.

The Chinese-American Cigarette Co., Ltd., was formed by R. J. Reynolds Tobacco International, Inc., and two Chinese partners in Xiamen.

The new company has a total investment of U.S. $21 million of which 50 percent came from RJR.

The joint venture will initially produce four brands – Camel, Winston, Golden Bridge, and Sprint. Five-sixths of the total output will be sold within China and the rest will be exported (October 31, 1988).

Domestic Gum Getting American Flavor

As a Sino-American joint venture, its partners are the Harbin No. 3 Sweet Factory and Warner-Lambert, with U.S. $4.9 million investment. The Harbin factory will provide the land, the buildings, and some equipment, while Warner-Lambert will provide the machinery and technology necessary to gum base, gum, and confectionaries. The chewing gum will be made from materials all grown or made in China.

Test sales were conducted at Beijing Friendship Store, where foreigners were surprised that they could get chewing gum to suit their taste in China (April 10, 1988).

Singer to Make and Sell Machines in China

Singer Sewing Machine Corp., Inc., and the Hua Nan Sewing Machine Industrial Co., of Guangzhou have announced the formation of an equity joint venture for the manufacture and sale of Singer Sewing Machines in China and for export.

The factory is scheduled to go into production by the end of March 1989. Initial goals are for the production of 300,000 consumer and artisan straight-stitch machines and 100,000 zig-zag machines annually.

Singer machines were first introduced to China in 1883. Its Chinese operations closed in 1941 because of war conditions (January 15, 1989).

2

Characteristics of the China Market

Population

China is a unified country comprising many different nationalities. The majority is Han; there are fifty-five other nationalities.

According to the 1982 census, China has a total population of 1,031,882,511 persons (51.5 percent m/48.5 percent f). The population of the Han nationality in China's twenty-nine provinces, municipalities, and autonomous regions (not including Taiwan Province and Jinmen and Mazu Islands in Fujian Province) is 936,703,824, or 93.3 percent.* The total population of all the other nationalities is 67,233,254, or 6.7 percent.

---

*Hainan Island's population of six million was included in the figures for Guangdong Province.

Population and Area of China's Provinces, Municipalities, and Autonomous Regions (1982 Census)

Province, Municipality, or Autonomous Region	Population	Area (square km)
Beijing Municipality	9,230,687	16,807
Tianjin Municipality	7,764,141	11,305
Hebei Province	53,005,875	187,700
Shanxi Province	25,291,389	156,300
Inner Mongolia Autonomous Region	19,274,279	1,183,000
Liaoning Province	35,721,693	145,700
Jilin Province	22,560,053	180,000
Heilongjiang Province	32,665,546	469,000
Shanghai Municipality	11,859,748	6,185
Jiangsu Province	60,521,114	102,600
Zhejiang Province	38,884,603	102,000
Anhui Province	49,665,724	139,900
Fujian Province	25,931,106	120,000
Jiangxi Province	33,184,827	166,600
Shandong Province	74,419,054	153,300
Henan Province	74,422,739	167,000
Hubei Province	47,804,150	187,000
Hunan Province	54,008,851	210,000
Guangdong Province	59,299,220	212,000
Guangxi Zhuang Autonomous Region	36,420,960	236,200
Sichuan Province	99,713,310	570,000
Guizhou Province	28,552,997	176,300
Yunnan Province	32,553,817	394,000
Tibet Autonomous Region	1,892,393	1,228,400
Shaanxi Province	28,904,423	206,000
Gansu Province	19,569,261	454,000
Qinghai Province	3,895,706	721,500
Ningxia Hui Autonomous Region	3,895,578	60,000
Xinjiang Uygur Autonomous Region	13,081,681	1,600,000
Taiwan Province	18,270,749	35,989

Population of China's Nationalities (1982 Census)

Nationalities	Population	Nationalities	Population
Han	936,703,824	Qiang	102,768
Zhuang	13,378,162	Daur	94,014
Hui	7,219,352	Jingpo	93,008
Uygur	5,957,112	Mulam	90,426
Yi	5,453,448	Xibe	83,629
Miao	5,030,897	Salar	69,102
Manchu	4,299,159	Blang	58,476
Tibetan	3,870,068	Gelo	53,802
Mongolian	3,411,657	Maonan	38,135
Tujia	2,832,743	Tajik	26,503
Bouyei	2,120,469	Nu	23,166
Korean	1,763,870	Pumi	20,441
Dong	1,425,100	Achang	20,411
Yao	1,402,676	Ewenki	19,343
Bai	1,131,124	Ozbek	12,453
Hani	1,058,836	Benglong	12,295
Kazak	907,582	Jing	11,995
Dai	839,797	Jino	11,974
Li	817,562	Yugur	10,569
Lisu	480,960	Bonan	9,027
She	368,832	Moinba	6,248
Lahu	304,174	Drung	4,682
Va	298,591	Oroqen	4,132
Shui	286,487	Tatar	4,127
Dongxiang	279,397	Russian	2,935
Naxi	245,154	Luoba	2,065
Tu	159,426	Gaoshan	1,549
Kirgiz	113,999	Hezhen	1,476

Other unclassified nationalities   879,201
Foreign nationals who have become Chinese citizens   4,842

Families (1982 Census)

Province, Municipality, or Autonomous Region	Number of families	Average family size
Beijing Municipality	2,352,300	3.7
Tianjin Municipality	1,921,113	3.9
Hebei Province	12,378,542	4.1
Shanxi Province	5,927,402	4.1
Inner Mongolia Autonomous Region	4,200,230	4.5
Liaoning Province	8,557,423	4.1
Jilin Province	5,083,025	4.4
Hailongjiang Province	7,157,986	4.5
Shanghai Municipality	3,151,778	3.6
Jiangsu Province	15,120,826	3.9
Zhejiang Province	9,604,404	4.0
Anhui Province	10,522,780	4.6
Fujian Province	5,170,364	4.8
Jiangxi Province	6,532,617	4.9
Shandong Province	17,390,448	4.2
Henan Province	15,365,407	4.7
Hubei Province	10,158,448	4.5
Hunan Province	12,339,618	4.2
Guangdong Province	11,962,218	4.8
Guangxi Zhuang Autonomous Region	6,938,850	5.1
Sichuan Province	22,870,671	4.2
Guizhou Province	5,687,232	4.9
Yunnan Province	6,140,974	5.2
Tibet Autonomous Region	324,679	5.1
Shaanxi Province	6,154,612	4.5
Gansu Province	3,756,501	5.1
Qinghai Province	722,882	5.2
Ningxia Hui Autonomous Region	742,047	5.1
Xinjiang Uygur Autonomous Region	2,938,408	4.3

Education Level, per 1,000 (1982 Census)

Province, Municipality, or Autonomous Region	College graduate	College	High school	Junior/ middle school	Primary school
Bejing Municipality	36	13	176	291	262
Tianjin Municipality	16	7	133	285	308
Hebei Province	3	1	75	193	364
Shanxi Province	4	2	74	219	388
Inner Mongolia Autonomous Region	4	1	75	193	328
Liaoning Province	7	3	93	276	357
Jilin Province	6	2	108	209	360
Heilongjiang Province	5	2	94	222	355
Shanghai Municipality	24	11	203	280	252
Jiangsu Province	5	2	70	201	326
Zhejiang Province	3	1	52	178	394
Anhui Province	3	1	40	142	297
Fujian Province	5	1	57	126	363
Jiangxi Province	3	1	55	133	386
Shandong Province	3	1	59	177	337
Henan Province	2	1	63	192	312
Hubei Province	4	2	75	187	356
Hunan Province	3	1	65	173	430
Guangdong Province	4	1	79	169	406
Guangxi Zhuang Autonomous Region	3	1	65	157	388
Sichuan Province	3	1	40	155	414
Guizhou Province	3	1	30	114	288
Yunnan Province	2	1	28	102	293
Tibet Autonomous Region	4	1	12	36	165
Shaanxi Province	6	2	79	194	327
Gansu Province	4	1	63	122	277
Qinghai Province	7	1	51	140	257
Ningxia Hui Autonomous Region	5	1	53	155	257
Xinjiang Uygur Autonomous Region	5	2	64	175	338

Languages

Spoken Chinese and Its Dialects

The Chinese language, also known as *hanyu*, usually refers to the standard language and its various dialects used by the majority nationality. Most of the minority nationalities have their own languages.

Chinese subdivides into the following dialects, which in their spoken form are mutually unintelligible:

Northern dialect (*beifanghua*).   This is the most widely spoken dialect in China, and forms the basis of *putonghua* ("common speech," sometimes called Mandarin), the official language of the People's Republic of China and the lingua franca of the Han nationality.

Wu dialect.   This dialect is spoken in the Shanghai region, southeastern Jiangsu Province and most of Zhejiang Province.

Xiang dialect.   The Xiang dialect is spoken by the inhabitants of Hunan Province (with the exception of the northwestern area).

Gan dialect.   Gan is spoken throughout Jiangxi Province (with the exception of the area bordering the Changjiang River and the southern area), and in southeastern Hubei Province.

Kejia (Hakka) dialect. This is the dialect spoken in parts of Guangdong, Guangxi, Fujian, and Jiangxi provinces.

Northern Min dialect.   This dialect is spoken in parts of northern Fujian and Taiwan provinces.

Southern Min dialect.   This is the dialect spoken throughout southern Fujian Province as well as in the Chaozhou and Shantou districts of Guangdong Province; in parts of Hainan Island; and throughout most of Taiwan Province.

Yue dialect (Cantonese).   The Yue dialect is spoken throughout central and southwestern Guangdong Province as well as in the southeastern part of the Guangxi Zhuang Autonomous Region.

The Written Language

The Chinese language is written in the form of symbols usually referred to as characters. They have an age-old history and a complex structure, and are extremely rich in variety. Originating approximately 6,000 years ago, they constitute one of the world's earliest written languages.

Although the Chinese dialects are diversified, the written language is universally understood among the literate populace.

The Traditional Solar Calendar and Seasonality

The Twenty-Four Solar Terms

Spring	1. Beginning of Spring	February 4 or 5
	2. Rain Water	February 19 or 20
	3. Waking of Insects	March 5 or 6
	4. Spring Equinox	March 20 or 21
	5. Pure Brightness (*Qingming*)	April 4 or 5
	6. Grain Rain	April 20 or 21
Summer	7. Beginning of Summer	May 5 or 6
	8. Grain Full	May 21 or 22
	9. Grain in Ear	June 5 or 6
	10. Summer Solstice	June 21 or 22
	11. Slight Heat	July 7 or 8
	12. Great Heat	July 23 or 24
Autumn	13. Beginning of Autumn	August 7 or 8
	14. Limit of Heat	August 23 or 24
	15. White Dew	September 7 or 8
	16. Autumnal Equinox	September 23 or 24
	17. Cold Dew	October 8 or 9
	18. Frost's Descent	October 23 or 24
Winter	19. Beginning of Winter	November 7 or 8
	20. Slight Snow	November 22 or 23
	21. Great Snow	December 7 or 8
	22. Winter Solstice	December 21 or 22
	23. Slight Cold	January 5 or 6
	24. Great Cold	January 20 or 21

This calendar is an important tool for marketing and advertising seasonal commodities. It reflects the Chinese people's attitudes with respect to their capricious climate. For instance, a Shanghai rubber shoe factory advertised in the February 19, 1986 issue of *Xin Min Evening News,* Shanghai with the single headline *Today Is Rain Water* (see chart), a message sufficient to convince great numbers of readers to buy rubber rain shoes.

Some Important Festivals

Chinese Lunar New Year.   This festival, also called the Spring Festival, was and still is the most widely celebrated festival throughout the whole of China. During the three-day holiday, people are busy visiting relatives and friends. Business is brisk in shops and restaurants. Vendors customarily present customers with promotional calendars containing illustrations symbolic of "happiness" or "longevity."

Mid-Autumn Festival.   The Mid-Autumn Festival falls on the fifteenth day of the eighth lunar month, precisely in the middle of autumn, when the moon is at its greatest distance from the earth and at peak brightness. People exchange presents, mostly pears, grapes, pomegranates, and moon cakes. The round shape of these objects symbolizes not only the moon but also the unity of the family.

Other Festivals.   There are over seventy well-known festivals celebrated by minorities in China. The best known include the Miao New Year Festival, the Dai Water-Splashing Festival, the Yi Torch Festival, the Dong Fireworks Festival, the Mongolian Nadam Fair, the Tibetan New Year Festival, and the Lisu Poles and Swords Festival. All these festivals have a strong local flavor and are quite interesting. They generally consist largely of entertainments, sports activities, and an extraordinary amount of buying and selling.

X Demographic Trends and Buying Behavior
An Aging Population

The world's population is growing old. According to world standards, a country in which 7 percent of the population is over sixty-five or 10 percent is over sixty may be said to have an elderly population.

In 1985, China's population over sixty reached 87 million, about 22 percent of the world total for people sixty and over.

The Shanghai figure is 1.65 million people over sixty, or 13.4 percent of the city's total population (figures from *Xin Min Evening News*, September 23, 1987).

The Older Generation

Pension payments to retired persons in China will amount to 9.3 percent of the total wages paid in 1983, and will go up to 15 percent in the year 2,000. Clearly, older people are important consumers. In larger cities, there are already specialty shops supplying clothing and daily necessities for older people. Nutritive foods, beverages, and medicines are key commodities in the older-person market and may likewise merit consideration for the seniors specialty format.

Tianjin's elderly are spending more now than they did when they were younger. The annual per-capita cost of living for senior citizens is 1,067 yuan a year and they spend 22 percent more on food than the average family in the city. Although they have retired, 26 percent have found other jobs, and their salaries along with support from children compensate for income lost by retirement (*China Daily*, August 26, 1987).

The Younger Generation

Young workers in Shanghai are spending their money in more diverse ways than in the past, according to a survey by the newspaper *China Youth News*.

Salaries, bonuses, and subsidies are the three main sources of income for young workers. According to the survey, workers under age thirty average 80–90 yuan (U.S. $22–25) a month. They spend it mainly in six fields.

1. Meals and health care account for one-quarter of their income. More and more young workers also buy expensive health tonics.

2. Clothes and daily necessities—20 percent for men, 30 percent for women.

3. Social activities, such as dating expenses, amount to at least 10 yuan a month.

4. Entertainment and leisure spending—on films, newspapers, and sightseeing—is increasing.

5. Savings are kept mostly to spend later on expensive commodities, such as washing machines, tape recorders, or color TVs. The survey found many are attracted by prizes offered by banks for deposits. One young worker put his whole 360-yuan bonus into a bank for that reason.

6. Child care requires more than 50 yuan a month per child (most Chinese families have only one child; figures from *China Daily*, August 21, 1986).

Young parents seem willing to spend when buying dresses for their children, giving preferences to two-piece costumes that are embroidered nicely and laced. People in Shanghai have a tradition of buying dresses for children on holidays and on their birthdays. They are now demanding good quality children's clothing not only in novel styles, but also in beautiful colors.

The Angel Children's Clothing Store, a well-known shop in Shanghai, sold more than 4,000 children's cat fur overcoats in the winter season of 1986, each costing 60–70 yuan (figures from *China Daily*, June 6, 1987).

Luxury Spending

"Whereas the Chinese used to dream of buying a bicycle or a watch, today many have more money to buy TVs, refrigerators—and electric organs.

"A leading department store in Shanghai reports that it has sold about 300 electric organs daily this year. The average price of the instrument is U.S. $40, or what an ordinary worker earns in a month and a half" (figures from *Advertising Age*, October 27, 1986).

The Swiss-made Rado Watch is the first foreign advertiser in *Wen Hui Pao*, Shanghai. It is an expensive item. A watch store in Beijing imported 100 Rado Watches at 4,000 yuan each and was sold out. Twenty more Rado watches priced at 8,950 yuan each were sold out too. The buyers included individual operators, retired *cadres*, and technologists (figures from *Economic Daily*, January 22, 1988).

The price of Hazeline Snow face cream is six times that of domestically made Double Maid. A small bottle of Malaysian-made Yung Fang face cream is sold at 9 yuan. Seven hundred bottles are sold daily by Shanghai No. 1 department store. The sales of imported cosmetics accounts for one-third of total cosmetics sales. The sales volume of cosmetics at Shanghai No. 2 Department Store reached 150,000 yuan a month because they sold high-price imported cosmetics.

There are more than 1,000 cosmetics manufacturers all over China, with an annual output of over 10 billion yuan. Some articles are of good quality. Cosmetics advertising occupies a certain percentage (figures from *Wen Hui Pao*, January 8, 1988).

A Survey of National Character

A survey was conducted in 324 of the country's 365 cities by the China Research Center for the Promotion of Scientific and Technological Development, a consulting agency under the State Science and Technology Commission, and by the China Institute of Social Surveys under the State Commission of Restructuring the Economic System.

A total of 4,244 people, selected to represent the country's urban population structure, responded to the questionnaire. The surveyors listed the following ten adjectives, from which the respondents were asked to select three that they thought best describe the national character: industrious, frugal, realistic, humane, gregarious, intelligent, adventurous, conservative, obedient, and concerned about saving face.

About half of the respondents chose "industrious" and "frugal," and more than a third selected "realistic," "conservative," and "obedient." Only 18.6 percent of the people preferred "intelligent," and only 2.7 percent chose "adventurous," the adjective chosen least.

Most people who chose "conservative," "obedient," and "concerned about saving face" are teachers, engineers, and students, of whom a majority are young (*China Daily*, September 28, 1987).

From the Business Pages

Ten Wants and Needs of the Well-Off Farmer

A report sent to the Central Communist Party from Feng Xin County, Jiangxi Province reflected the following ten most requested goods and services among well-off farmers.

---

1. High-quality heavy-load bicycles

2. Small agricultural machinery

3. Training in agricultural technology

4. Chemical fertilizer and farm insecticide

5. Sideline processing equipment

6. Commodity circulation systems for farm by-products

7. Varied and colorful cultural life

8. High-grade ready-made garments

9. High-class confectionery goods

10. Touring opportunities within China

The report gave per-capita savings of the Shanghai rural residents as 621.03 yuan — the highest in all China. And it showed these farmers to be potential customers for a great range of commodities (*Sin Wen Bao*, October 1, 1987).

Predicted Spending for Rural Families

According to a survey made by the State Statistical Bureau among 38,283 rural families in 682 counties, the demand for durable consumer goods per 100 households in 1988 is predicted as follows:

Items	Demand	% increase over 1986
Electric fan	12.4	220
TV set	8.6	81
Tape recorder	4.1	110
Radio	2.3	10
Washing machine	2.9	160
Refrigerator	0.48	430
Camera	0.22	230
Bicycle	22.3	110
Sewing machine	7.9	160
Wristwatch	19.8	21

Source: *Economic Daily*, January 9, 1988.

Rural Market Enlivens Economy

According to the State Statistical Bureau, the rural market flourished in the first half of 1987. Total retail sales reached 1,549 billion yuan, an increase of 19.6 percent over the same period of 1986.

Sales of capital goods increased by the percentages shown over the same period of 1986:

Pesticide	+14.1
Chemical fertilizer	+11.3
Plastic film	+36.5
Large tractors	+65.6
Power machinery	+37.7

Source: *China Industry and Commerce Gazette*, August 4, 1987.

Overall, the farm machinery industry in China has managed to expand its production. In the first seven months of 1987, farm machinery enterprises increased their output value by 29.8 percent over the same period in 1986 (*China Daily*, September 22, 1987).

Rural Poverty Eradicated

Nearly 80 percent of the estimated 500 million impoverished rural people in China have been lifted above the poverty line in the past eight years.

Statistics show that the social output value of 664 key poverty-stricken counties topped 107.01 billion yuan in 1986 and their per-capita annual income reached 217.8 yuan, an increase of 175.5 yuan over 1980 (*China Daily*, September 22, 1987).

Cave Villagers Turn Over a New Leaf

Dazhai, once a production brigade in north China's Shanxi Province, used to be called a "national pace-setter" because they managed to develop an egalitarian collective rural economy before the 1980s.

Now, according to statistics, the village's total income reached 630,000 yuan (U.S. $170,000) in 1986, three times the 1978 figure. Local per-capita income jumped 340 percent during the same period.

Dazhai people still live in caves like they did ten years ago, but the worn-out furniture and identical mugs and jars have been replaced by fashionable sofas and wardrobes in different colors and designs. In every home can be found TV sets, sewing machines, tape-recorders, and refrigerators (*China Daily*, September 14, 1987).

3

Applying Western Techniques to Marketing in China

Historically, Western marketing techniques have proved to be not only applicable, but quite successful, in China. The work of the top advertising agencies in the 1930s, for example, closely followed the American style. Consumer commodities, such as Listerine toothpaste, successfully ran the original ads, simply making ethnic alterations in the models.

Often, Western techniques have been applied in advance of the theories explaining them. For instance, the Hua Ming Tobacco Company opened around 1941. A medium-sized cigarette company, it did not have the advertising budget or sales force to compete with the huge Hua Cheng Tobacco Company or Nanyang Brothers Tobacco Company on the overall market. So the owners decided to concentrate their marketing efforts. Hua Ming selected Suzhou, Wuxi, and Kun Shan, and supplied calendars to every room of the hotels in these cities. After some supplementary giveaways Hua Ming's products dominated these cities. Of course, Hua Ming was enjoying the fruits of market segmentation and target market, techniques the owners had never heard of.

Where Is Your Target Market?

Before Liberation, foreign commodities were mainly sold in larger cities, such as Shanghai, Tianjin, and Guangzhou. Now the China market is much larger. The users of capital goods (production) are scattered all over the country. So newspapers have national circulation and direct mail (DM) can be used, while Central TV and Central radio broadcasting and trade magazines will be increasingly effective.

For subsistence goods or consumer goods, market segmentation is more important. Efforts may be concentrated in larger or coastal cities initially and then gradually shifted to the interior cities.

Market Research and Market Survey

Market segmentation, of course, must be based on market research. As Chapter 1 demonstrates, a good deal of secondary data can be collected. So far, some advertising agencies can undertake market research, although there are no commercial agencies that specialize in furnishing external secondary data. Government statistics can be collected from newspaper and magazine articles.

For primary data, interviews and observation methods should be used. The telephone interview will become more practicable as China's consumer telecommunications attains par with the West.

Market surveys are furnishing increasingly valuable information. For instance, Kentucky Fried Chicken is to set up a joint-venture snack restaurant in Beijing. To prepare for it, Hong Kong-based Interpublic Jardine (China) Ltd., the advertising agent of American Snack, entrusted the Beijing Advertising Corporation to run a chicken-tasting survey among the pedestrians in Beijing seeking their opinions on Chinese chicken fried the American way.

With the rapid increase in international marketing in China since 1979, several large advertising firms have augmented their services with market research departments. Among these firms are Beijing Advertising Corporation, Shanghai Advertising Corporation, Guangdong Advertising Corporation, the China International Advertising Corporation, and Shanghai Industrial Consultants.

Originally, Japan led others in selling products in China; these corporations' main clients were Japanese. Today, these agencies extend their services to firms in Switzerland, the United States, Great Britain, West Germany, Finland, and Hong Kong. Their most commonly requested services are organizing panel discussions and conducting household interviews.

Marketing and Promotional Mix

The marketing mix and promotional mix concepts in marketing management are applicable in China.

In the marketing mix, product planning, pricing, distribution, and promotion are all important factors. Product planning includes packaging, and outfitting the product with an effective Chinese name. Sometimes the packaging is designed by an American advertising agency. One successful instance is Orange Tang. The package and mark are very appealing, especially with the wording "Selected by NASA for U.S. Space Flights."

A good Chinese name for the product is helpful to sales. For instance, Gillette used the Chinese name *Jili* (lucky). Coca-Cola used the four Chinese characters *ke kuo ke le* (palatable and enjoyable). Pepsi-Cola's Chinese name is *bai shi ke le* (makes everything enjoyable). These are good names because the Chinese respond to associations with luck and good fortune.

Orange Tang, advertised as a "fresh-squeezed orange taste instant drink," has the Chinese name *gu zhen* (fruit treasure).

Changsha Refrigerator Factory uses Italian technology in its manufacturing. It uses *Zhongyi* as a brand name, which means both "Sino-Italian" and "satisfactory" or "to one's liking."

In the promotion mix, there is a trend in the United States toward spending more money on promotion than on advertising. In China, the term *promotion* is accepted in an all-inclusive sense. In his book *Marketing Management*, Victor P. Buell defined the following "elements of promotion," all applicable in China:

- Advertising—any paid message presented through TV, radio, magazine, newspapers, or billboards by an identified source

- Personal selling—sales contacts made with trade, end users, or influencers (nonbuyers who influence brand or product selection) by company salespersons

- Sales promotion—any other communication or persuasive device; a catch-all term which includes things as diverse as coupons, product samples, cents-off deals, displays, trade show booths, contests, product brochures

- Publicity—any unpaid-for mention of a company, brand, or product by media

Because China is a vast country, advertising is sometimes more economical than personal selling. The September 15, 1987 issue of

China Industry and Commerce Gazette, an official organ of the State Administration of Industry and Commerce, reported that at a forty-person plastic machinery factory in Yong Qing County, Hebei Province, products stockpiled as high as 300,000 yuan because there was no sales force. To sell their product, five or six salespersons would have been necessary, at a total cost of 30–36,000 yuan annually. By spending 8,000 yuan for advertising in newspapers, TV, and radio instead, the monthly capacity was regularly sold out.

Advertising Always Pays

In China, as in the West, advertising is an investment, and not an expense. Today many Chinese enterprisers still do not realize this.

Some notable cases prove the effectiveness of advertising in China since its resumption in 1979.

Japanese Commodities

Japanese Dentsu started sending consultants to China as soon as state-to-state relations were normalized in 1972. The China offices of such Japanese advertising agencies as Dentsu and Hakuhodo were set up in Beijing. And Japanese advertising in China occupied 75 percent of foreign advertising for the last few years. When the commodities were not sold as yet on the market, advertisements were used to foster brand awareness. This was called "investment advertising."

An often-quoted news article tells of a Chinese visitor to the United States who wanted to buy a television set. He preferred to buy a Sony instead of an American-made device, although the latter was quite famous in the U.S. and of proven quality. He knew Sony better through advertising, however.

China has an old idiom: "Whosoever enters first is master." This has proven most true with Japanese advertising.

The following figures show the increase in sales of one Japanese copier that was backed up by investment advertising.

1981	1,426
1982	3,133
1983	19,605
1984	24,322
1985	90,066

In the following categories, the percentage of Japanese-made commodities are as follows:

color TV	87.83%
refrigerator	68.40%
car	63%

American Commodities

Kodak entered the China market quite early, and it had been a famous brand on the market before Liberation. In 1986, during the World Cup Soccer Competition, China International Advertising Corporation started an advertising campaign with Kodak based on making a forecast of the winners. Originally, about 200,000 people were expected to enter the contest. Actually, about 2.4 million people participated in the campaign. A survey made in Beijing shows that fifty out of 100 consumers know and would use Kodak film.

Chinese Commodities

A toothpaste factory in Liuzhou, Guangxi Province faced bankruptcy in 1981 because of inefficient management and a product that was not competitive. After improvements were made in management and market research was undertaken, advertising helped the 1982 production to increase 83.3 percent over 1981; 1983 production increased 113.4 percent over 1982. This brand became the second most popular in a field of over ten. In the first half of 1986, though, when production could not meet the market demand for this brand, advertising was cut back and sales dropped right away. When advertising again was stepped up in the latter part of 1986, increased sales objectives were met.

Sales of West Lake TV sets increased 3,000 percent from 1980 to 1986 after an increase in advertising expenditure of 1,000 percent during the same period.

A freezer factory in Yantai, Shandong Province advertised in coastal cities in 1982: 3,757 users were added. In 1984, they advertised in other cities and 355 users were added. A survey showed that 35 percent of the new users were secured through advertising.

When Tsingtao Beer entered the American market in 1978, 20,000 cases were shipped. In 1986, one million cases were shipped—a fifty-fold increase. Notwithstanding the high quality of the product, advertising played an important role. The sole agent in America advertised Tsingtao Beer through TV, radio, newspapers, and magazines. It is said that the advertising expenditure even exceeded the agency's commission.

Temple of Heaven Essential Balm is a small export item. Research showed that in Mali, Africa, when people catch cold or have a mosquito bite, they use balm. An advertising campaign was launched in cooperation with Ogilvy & Mather, and Chinese-made Temple of Heaven Essential Balm became a leading brand in Mali.* In a five-day negotiation made through China Health Care Medicine Group, a $215,000 contract was signed.

*The brand name was subsequently changed to "Dragon and Tiger Balm."

4

How to Enter the China Market

Companies still waiting for the right moment to enter the China market have a number of pathways that they may consider.

China's Import and Export Corporations

There are many import and export corporations with head offices in Beijing and branch offices in important cities. Contact any of the corporations on the following list for consideration of your product or service.

China National Textiles Import and Export Corporation

China National Native Produce and Animal By-products Import and Export Corporation

China National Arts and Crafts Import and Export Corporation

China National Cereals, Oils & Foodstuffs Import and Export Corporation

China National Metals & Minerals Import and Export Corporation

China National Machinery Import and Export Corporation

China National Chemicals Import and Export Corporation

China National Light Industrial Products Import and Export Corporation

China National Medicines and Health Products Import and Export Corporation

China National Machinery & Equipment Import and Export Corporation

China National Film Export and Import Corporation

China National Packaging Import and Export Corporation

China National Coal Import and Export Corporation

China National Nonferrous Metals Import and Export Corporation

China National Technical Import Corporation

China Council for the Promotion of International Trade

The head office of the China Council for the Promotion of International Trade is situated in Beijing, with sub-councils in the various provinces and autonomous regions. Its head office has access to the China International Exhibition Center in Beijing and a department to recommend current literature and samples of foreign commodities.

Denmark put on a special show at the China International Exhibition Center in Beijing in June 1987 to familiarize Chinese visitors with Denmark's own vast agriculture. About forty-two companies or enterprises exhibited their products or models with the hope of establishing cooperative or business relationships with Chinese counterparts.

Denmark China Food System, with its four member companies, has provided China with its "best equipment for processing agricultural products" and is also working on a joint venture for quick-freezing vegetables in Tianjin, China's third largest municipality, directly under the State Council.

Exhibitions are effective to introduce commodities. Hong Kong-based Adsale Exhibition Services organizes regular exhibitions, many of which are supported by CCPIT.

Finding the *Hongniang,* or Go-Between

Hongniang is the name of a maidservant in a Chinese classical drama who helps her mistress break the yoke of the feudal ethical code and marry her lover. Hence this name is given to those who act as go-between in helping two parties achieve a common objective.

The following corporations and organizations are all willing to act as a "hongniang" in finding the right importer for foreign companies.

- China Industrial and Commercial Economic Consulting Corporation (CICECC), recently established by China Federation of Industry and Commerce in Beijing

- The Consulting Department of the Shanghai Federation of Industry and Commerce, and the Federation's Foreign Trade Section

- Shanghai Industry and Commerce Development Corporation

In addition, the Shanghai Foreign Trade Corporation has a consulting corporation, which can evaluate foreign commodities as potential imports. A certain amount of service charge will be made.

Public Relations and Sales Promotion

Public relations is a new thing to China. But public relations techniques work in China. Hill and Knowlton Asia Ltd. established an office in Beijing in 1984. By 1986, the company had offered over thirty media-oriented services for its clients, including United Airlines, Electronic Data Systems of General Motors, and the New York Stock Exchange.

When the American film *Love Story* was shown in Beijing in March 1986, Hollywood moviemakers and China's Film Import/ Export Corporation gave a joint press conference in the Chinese capital. Hill and Knowlton was the consultant to both sides of the project.

One of Hill and Knowlton's services is to distribute press releases on behalf of foreign clients to Chinese media, government organizations, and enterprises. These clients include International Wool Secretariat, Allied-Signal China, and Lufthansa.

One way of introducing commodities to the China market is to use sample promotions. French Remy Martin, Nescafe, and Orange Tang all used this method. Coca-Cola had a booth in the hall of the Third World Advertising Congress held in Beijing in June 1987, offering free Coke in cups, and flashy leaflets printed in both English and Chinese.

Another sound method is sponsoring. Mobil sponsored China photographs by Hiroji Kubota in Beijing, Shanghai, and Hong Kong. Newspaper ads and posters were used. The newspaper ad included the following citation:

> Sponsored by the China Exhibition Agency, Ministry of Culture. Organized by The International Center of Photographs, New York City. Made possible by a grant from Mobil Oil Corporation.

The president, vice president, and senior officers of Mobil visited Beijing in March 1987 and held a press conference about the opening of the photograph exhibition. The president said that when the Mobil sign next appeared along their highways, he hoped that the Chinese people would see it as a symbol of friendship (*Economic Daily*, March 19, 1987).

Upon winning the 1987 Motor Car Rally, Toyota Motor Corporation placed a big advertisement in newspapers to thank the supporters. This ad belongs in the public relations advertising category.

Public relations continues to grow as an industry in China. Today, almost all Chinese enterprises and factories realize the importance of promoting and maintaining a good public image and have set up public relations departments. More than 300 factories have established public relations departments in Shanghai alone.

An example is the Shanghai Watch Factory, whose output accounts for 25 percent of the national total. Plant director Qi Delin attributes this success to the public relations department.

Showrooms and Service Centers

For products like automobiles and farm machinery, a showroom is quite necessary. Before Liberation, major international automobile companies all had showrooms in China, employing salespersons to persuade potential buyers to have a close look and take a drive. "Seeing is believing" proved to be helpful in selling. Now motor cars and farm machinery are being displayed once again in showrooms, but many brands of commodities are shown together because the showrooms are the offices of agents.

Another important step is to establish service centers. Omega watch appointed a watch store as its service center in Shanghai, Sanyo established its own service center, and Citizen watch has service centers in Beijing, Shanghai, Guangzhou, and other cities. Ricoh announced in a newspaper ad that there are twenty-eight service centers and Shanghai Volkswagen advertises that it has thirty-two SVW authorized service stations across China.

Competition Research

The old saying is, "Know the enemy and know yourself, and you can fight a hundred battles with no danger of defeat." As competition is very keen on the market, knowing what your competitors are doing will often determine advertising strategy, especially where—as in the case of daily-use articles—a buyer's market is developing. In China, competition is encouraged if it is in the cause of quality and service. Two market conditions will illustrate some current competition analysis.

The Soft Drink Market

There are many soft drinks on the market. From the United States, Coca-Cola, Pepsi-Cola, 7UP, and Royal Crown all compete on the market. The retail prices (in 1987) in Shanghai compare as shown.

Unit	Coca-Cola (355 ml)	Pepsi-Cola (355 ml)	7UP (355 ml)	Royal Crown (350 ml)
Bottle	5.20 yuan	4.80 yuan	no	no
Can	2.00 yuan	1.85 yuan	2.00 yuan	1.70 yuan

The difference in prices may be due to cost, contents, transportation, etc.

According to the leaflet distributed by Coca-Cola, the company is not a traditional multinational company. It is a multilocal company which assists its local partners in developing their market. In China, Coca-Cola works with Chinese economic units who own and operate their bottling plants; these Chinese companies produce all the Coca-Cola, Fanta, and Sprite sold in China, and retain the benefits. Coca-Cola appeared for the first time in China in the 1920s, with bottling operations owned and operated by local Chinese bottlers in Tianjin, Shanghai, and Qingdao. In 1933, the Shanghai bottler became the largest soft drink-producing plant outside the United States.

Sales of Coca-Cola in China recommenced in late 1978. The first shipment of Coca-Cola was sent from Hong Kong in January 1979, and Coke became one of the first international consumer products to be available in the People's Republic of China after inception of the country's open door policy.

The total annual production capacity in early 1987 stood at 90,000 tons of beverage (14 million cases) in bottles and 65,000 tons of beverage (7.5 million cases) in cans. TV, newspaper, billboard, showcard, and P.O.P. are used, and the company sponsors many activities. It enjoys the lead position on the market.

Pepsi operates two joint-venture plants in China: the Shenzhen City Happiness Soft Drink Factory was opened in 1981 and Guangzhou Pepsi-Cola Soft Drink Factory opened in 1986. A third plant, the Fuzhou Pepsi-Cola Soft Drink Factory, was scheduled to open in January 1988.

Pepsi also wants to complete agreements with Beijing and Shenzhen to establish new joint-venture bottling facilities in the two cities.

The Shanghai plant has a production capacity of 144 million bottles and cans per year, while the Guangzhou factory produces 96 million bottles and cans of Pepsi-Cola, 7UP, and Mirinda Orange soft drinks a year for domestic consumption.

Pepsi-Cola is sold alongside Coca-Cola in food stores. So is 7UP and Royal Crown. People know Pepsi-Cola now, but 7UP and Royal Crown are not so familiar with the Chinese, because they are not extensively advertised and entered the China market only in recent years. The Chinese name of 7UP is *qi xi*, (seven happiness) and Royal Crown is *huang guan,* a literal translation of *Royal Crown.*

There are Chinese-made colas on the market. Chongqing-based Tianfu Cola is made solely from natural ingredients and without caffeine as the advertisement says. It is sold at 1.30 yuan for a standard 355-ml can. It has bottlers in twenty-five provinces and municipalities with seventy-five branch factories. It is often catered at State banquets. Tianfu Cola uses newspaper advertising and posters. There are about a dozen other Chinese-made colas such as Laoshan Cola, which is made in Qingdao and sells at a lower price than Coke. The shape of their 1.25-liter bottle copies the equivalent bottles used by Coca-Cola and Pepsi-Cola.

On the occasion of the third anniversary of the creation of Jianlibao, the sports drink that made its debut at the Olympic Games, the factory put a half-page advertisement in the August 28, 1987 issue of *China Daily*, saying that its annual output had reached 50,000 tons. Jianlibao is bottled in 355 ml cans, 250 ml glass bottles, and 1.25 L plastic bottles, and has been named the special beverage for State banquets.

The soft drink industry is a major item in the Seventh Five-Year Plan (1986–1990), and the industry has developed rapidly in recent years.

Statistics showed China's nonalcoholic drink output reached 1.84 million tons in 1986.

With its large population, China offers a vast potential market. Although soft drink production in recent years has registered a sharp growth, famous-brand soft drinks are still in short supply in many cities.

The increase in output is one thing, and brand preference is quite another. Advertising can play an important role in increasing the brand-awareness and market share.

The Toothpaste Market

There are more than ten brands of toothpaste on the market. Some are old brands, some are new. They are sold side by side from the store counters. All are domestically made. One brand, Maxam, is exported as well as sold in China. There is no foreign toothpaste on the market so far, and domestic competition is keen.

On the date of a recent, well-attended buyers' convention in Nanning, Guangxi Province, passengers arriving at the Nanning Railway Station found themselves surrounded by advertisements for medicated toothpastes. Banners proclaimed "Liang Mian Zhen Toothpaste Welcomes You!" while mobile sound systems blared toothpaste advertisements (from an article in *Economic Daily*, June 26, 1987).

Hangzhou-made Small White Rabbit toothpaste, marketed in the Rabbit year (according to the twelve animals used to symbolize the year in which a person is born), used advertising that appealed to youngsters. Its TV commercial took first prize in the first national competition organized by the TV commercial committee of the China Advertising Association.

Beijing-made Xi Bi Da Medicated Toothpaste became quite famous when it was marketed in 1978. But production took three years to meet demand, and by 1985, sales had declined sharply. One reason was that the advertising was not executed properly. Another was a simultaneous campaign for a feminine hygiene product that unfortunately bore the same name as the toothpaste.

At the same time when Xi Bi Da began to enter the market, many new brands made in Dandong, Qingdao, Tianjin, Liuzhou, and Chengdu all entered the market. Jie Yin, a brand produced by the Guangzhou Tube Factory, was made according to the prescription of First Military Hospital; this fact gave it prestige among consumers. Jie Yin used testimonial copy in its advertising. In 1984, the annual output reached 50 million packets, twenty-four times its first-year sales.

When Jie Yin was first marketed, the output of Guangzhou Tooth Paste Factory had already reached 66 million packets. If the Guangzhou Tooth Paste Factory had not turned down the prescription first offered to it by the First Military Hospital, there would not have been a market for Jie Yin.

Blue Sky of Tianjin was another success. When it was marketed, the factory sold through its own channels, backed up by advertising, and at the same time offered better terms to the stores. In addition, it increased its line to eighteen different kinds to meet the different market demands.

From the Business Pages

Challenge to Coca-Cola

Li Jingwei, 48, who has never been to school and can hardly read, is managing the Guangdong Sports Drink Company, which is expecting a turnover of 125 million yuan from its single product — the soft drink Jianlibao.

Says Li: "Coca-Cola has always dominated the world market, but now it's time for us to have a share in it."

A sports enthusiast, at 21, Li was made a deputy director of the sports commission of his home town in Sanshui County, Guangdong Province, and in 12 years made many friends in the sporting world. In 1974, he was appointed director of the Sanshui Winery and switched from producing spirits to brewing of beer. Li decided to develop a new product. In late 1983, after Li had devoted 18 hours a day over 10 months to his idea, China's first sports drink was born. It became China's official Olympic drink. In 1984 the output was 1,000 tons; the next year it reached 6,000 tons. Orders have reached 40,000 tons for 1987, which means an output value of more than 100 million yuan and a profit of more than 20 million yuan for the factory, which now has 600 employees.

Li spends a lot of money on advertising. In 1986 alone, the factory spent about 2 million yuan on advertising and sponsoring sport teams and tournaments.

Li is aiming at an output value of 1,000 million yuan to challenge Coca-Cola (*China Daily*, August 4, 1987).

Advertising in China is at least as old as the *huangzi*, traditional signs emblematic of the various trades, and the songs of itinerant peddlers. As the scope of economic activity in China increased, the use of advertising became more sophisticated.

The ads on the following pages illustrate a variety of advertising approaches. The selection is heavily weighted in favor of ads current in the 1920s and 1930s — the "golden age" of Chinese advertising, when the influx of Western consumer and luxury goods, and the attendant advertising, had great influence on the buying habits of the Chinese consumer.

Traditional signs, usually called *Huangzi*, were emblematic of a shop's trade.

Itinerant peddlers provided food, clothing, and amusement.

"There is a peddler selling. . . . His voice pitches very high and everytime he cries, all the hotel guests are surprised" (commentary on a Qing Dynasty folk song).

電話購貨
迅速經濟

購買東西，出門一次，既費時間，
又費車力，其實抵要打一個電
話通知各商店送貨到收款，
再簡便省事也沒有現在各商
店大都設有電話，他們都願意
聽候你的電話替你服務。

電話除了購貨
品之外，更有許多
用處，現代价已城
低，每月祇收六元
半，可免費打一百
次，新式家庭實在
不可不裝請即通
知本公司營業部
電話九四○九○，
即日裝置享受便
利舒適的現代生
活。

上海電話公司

30-36

Foreign-owned utility companies, like Shanghai Telephone,
advertised to encourage people to use their fledgling service.

Pyramid handkerchiefs was a regular advertiser in the 1930s.

The Chinese public was introduced to a host of consumer goods in the 1920s and 1930s, such as the Westinghouse refrigerator advertised here.

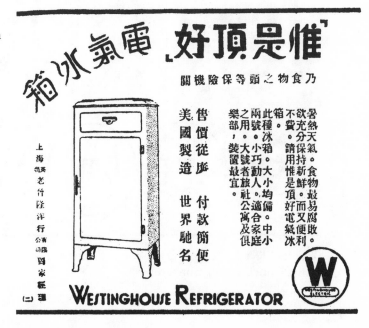

General Electric, Philips, Osram, and Tungsram merged to form the
China United Lamp Company.

Merchants pasted up posters from foreign countries. This ad was displayed on counters in cigarette shops.

Cover for a women's magazine, *Happy Home*, edited by the author in 1935.

Omega watch ad, circa 1938.

The use of models, or famous actresses, and the development of photography as an advertising tool went hand in hand in China, as elsewhere.

精品 化粧 佳是都 「四七一」 雪花精 古龍香水 香水精

德國「四七一」名廠之此化粧名品
色質之優美
是佳化粧名品
之都麗潔厚
在在超人一等歐
美閒秀之神品之
公認為美容之神品

注 凡美容上一之化粧
意 四七一」現均有名
中國國粉註冊

Nº4711.

香粉

"4711" Tosca

Print ad featuring beauty
products from a German
manufacturer.

Myrna Loy — for Max Factor.

O Cedar Wax Cream—one of many housekeeping products introduced into the China market.

The Bayer name has long been a familiar one to the Chinese consumer.

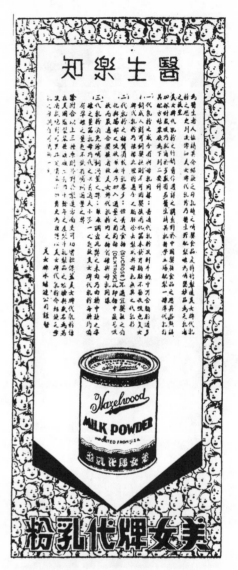

Bovril – a British-made beverage featured in this ad – also competed for advertising space on the sides and tops of streetcars.

"Hazelwood" – a brand of the American-owned Henningsen Produce Company, established in Shanghai in 1913.

"Sweetie Spearmint," another Henningsen product.

Bang Yi Peng, well-known commercial artist in the 1930s, created this ad.

Instead of salt, the Chinese learned to use toothpaste to brush their teeth.

With 10 cents, one could get three Polo Pens and samples of calligraphy.

This line drawing won first prize in the Shanghai Advertising Exhibition held in January 1987. Copy for the ad was written by Xu Bai Yi.

Ruby Cosmetics installed this ticket-selling counter at the Jin Jiang Amusement Park, Shanghai.

A Zhong Hua Toothpaste tube — to be displayed at the new Shanghai railway station.

Outdoor advertising — modern versions of a traditional approach, for Siemens and . . .

Casio products.

5

A New Era for Advertising in China

Commercial advertising resumed in China in the spring of 1979, when a Shanghai radio broadcast carried a spot announcement for a local photo studio.

Over the previous ten years, everyone had been wearing the blue or grey Mao dresses, male or female; women's hair was cut short, and not a smiling face could be seen. The manufacturing and distribution of commodities was strictly controlled through the state commercial departments. Advertising was treated as a capitalist token and totally banned.

After 1979, advertising as a business flourished in China.

Advertising Industry Growth

Year	1979	1981	1984	1985	1986	1987
Business volume (millions of yuan)	NA	150	360	600	845	1,120
Number of employees	NA	16,000	50,000	63,819	81,130	92,270
Number of agencies	10	2,100	4,077	6,054	6,944	8,225

In 1979, advertising agencies existed only in large cities such as Shanghai, Tianjin, Guangzhou, Nanjing, and Beijing. Shanghai had the most, with three: Shanghai Advertising and Decorating Corporation, Shanghai Advertising Corporation, and Shanghai Art-designing Company. In other cities, only one or two existed. By contrast, when a meeting was held in Guangzhou in October 1980, about ten companies were represented.

In 1986, the total advertising and business volume included U.S. $14,879,000 of foreign advertising.

Advertising Business Volume, 1986*

By media (%)		By commodity (%)	
Newspaper	30.3	Capital goods	32.0
Television	13.6	Daily use articles	21.4
Radio	4.2	Foodstuffs	8.5
Magazine	4.2	Medicine	7.6
Other	22.1	Cultural	6.3
		Other	24.2

*On February 6, 1982, a set of "Interim Regulations for Advertising" were promulgated by the State Council; "Regulations for Advertising Management" entered into force on December 1, 1987 (see Appendix II).

Advertising Business Volume, by Territory, 1986

Rank	Territory	Volume of business (10,000 yuan)
1	Guangdong Province	14,598.4
2	Beijing	14,535.8
3	Sichuan Province	12,589.3
4	Shanghai	8,617.0
5	Liaoning Province	7,428.6
6	Tianjin	7,159.7
7	Jiangsu Province	5,066.1
8	Shandong Province	3,777.8
9	Hubei Province	3,529.0
10	Zhejiang Province	3,007.6
11	Shaanxi Province	2,667.01
12	Heilongjiang Province	2,408.1
13	Fujian Province	2,136.7

14	Henan Province	2,072.07
15	Hunan Province	2,003.0
16	Anhui Province	1,972.4
17	Hebai Province	1,694.3
18	Jilin Province	1,047.8
19	Jiangxi Province	1,036.8
20	Guangxi Zhuang Autonomous Region	1,022.9
21	Shanxi Province	918.4
22	Xinjiang Uygur Autonomous Region	614.1
23	Yunnan Province	597.8
24	Gansu Province	552.4
25	Guizhou Province	482.8
26	Inner Mongolia Autonomous Region	400.5
27	Ningxia Hui Autonomous Region	178.8
28	Qinghai Province	140.0
	Tibet Autonomous Region	NA
	Taiwan Province	NA

Source: *China Features*, No. 6, p. 4, 1987.

Ten Leading Foreign Advertisers, 1986

Rank	Adver-tiser	TV	News-paper	Radio	Maga-zine	Billboard in Beijing	Total (U.S. $)
1	Toshiba	1,099,667	349,895	99,945	52,566	55,135	1,657,218
2	Hitachi	626,819	240,417			32,692	900,048
3	Mitsubishi	251,488	265,933	4,859	3,600	47,020	568,041
4	Konica	347,480	111,340		10,734	81,081	550,644
5	Philips	355,522	183,248		1,391	8,103	548,269
6	Canon	274,140	89,635		6,756	30,270	399,197
7	Ricoh	222,390	129,744			29,919	382,054
8	Nestlé	369,971					369,971
9	Maxwell	338,183					338,183
10	Kodak	284,495	19,459			27,243	331,197

Source: *China Features*, No. 3, p. 2, 1987.

Beijing Advertising Corporation compiled a list showing the expenditures of various foreign advertisers. TV advertising figures are combined totals for four major broadcast stations: Central TV, Beijing TV, Shanghai TV, and Guangdong TV. Radio broadcasting figures are totals combined from four major stations: Central People's Radio, Beijing People's Radio, Shanghai People's Radio, and Guangdong Radio. Other media totals are calculated according to the rate cards.

Ten Leading Foreign Advertisers Compared, 1986–1987

1986 (U.S. $m)		1987 (U.S. $m)	
Toshiba	1.66	Toshiba	1.1
Hitachi	0.90	Hitachi	0.66
Mitsubishi	0.57	NEC	0.59
Konica	0.55	Marlboro	0.56
Philips	0.55	Nestlé	0.36
Canon	0.40	Casio	0.34
Ricoh	0.38	Sumitomo Chemicals	0.32
Nestlé	0.37	Mitsubishi Heavy Industry	0.31
Maxwell House	0.34	Kodak	0.30
Kodak	0.33	Ricoh	0.30

Source: From Survey Research Group as published in *Media*, Hong Kong, December 16, 1988.

The Major Advertising Companies

China International Advertising Corporation (CIAC), Beijing

China International Advertising Corporation was established as an independent legal economic entity in September 1984. CIAC is affiliated with the Ministry of Foreign Economic Relations and Trade and specializes in the import and export advertising business.

This company lays particular emphasis on the study of strategic plans for business development. CIAC does its utmost to open up domestic and international markets for its foreign clients through diligent research.

CIAC is organized into six departments: national business, imports, business with Socialist countries, market research, market development, and design and creative.

On its Board of Directors are practically all of the presidents or vice presidents of Chinese import and export corporations. Besides the regular services, CIAC can arrange foreign economic and technical cooperation projects related to advertising. CIAC sponsored many exhibitions in 1986, including the International Office Equipment Exhibition, International Advertising Production

Technology and Equipment Exhibition and International Electric Products Exhibition.

Shanghai Advertising and Decorating Corporation

Shanghai Advertising and Decorating Corporation is the largest advertising corporation in China, with about 1,000 personnel. Its thirty-year history begins with the transformation movement in 1956, which amalgamated all the advertising agencies in Shanghai.

Besides the research, business, and design departments, market research and market development departments were set up in 1987. This corporation has clients from Japan, United States, Federal Republic of Germany, Canada, Holland, Hong Kong, and Macao. It is the publisher of the quarterly *China Advertising*.

Shanghai Advertising Corporation

Shanghai Advertising Corporation was founded in 1962 as a specialized advertising agency to handle import and export advertising. In addition to its research and creative departments, Shanghai Advertising carries an exhibitions department and its own printing factory. Its services include marketing research, public relations, advertising planning, creation, and production. Its annual turnover in the past twenty-five years increased an average 40 percent annually. The editorial department of the quarterly magazine *International Advertisement* is situated in Shanghai Advertising Corporation.

Other Large Agencies

There are about forty advertising agencies in other important provinces and cities that handle import advertising. Two worthy of note are China Resources Advertising Co., Ltd., Hong Kong, which handles overseas advertising in China, and Adsale Hong Kong, established 1977. Adsale offers China trade promotion services including exhibition, advertising, publishing, media representation, translation, printing, and direct response implementation.

Foreign Advertising Agents and Joint-Venture Advertising Agencies

Japanese Dentsu came first into China, starting offices in Beijing and Shanghai soon after advertising was resumed in 1979. The company set up the China Department of its Tokyo head office in March 1985 for specialized advertising transactions with China. Ten employees (including two Chinese) are working for the department. (Japanese Hakuhodo and Daiko also have offices in Beijing.)

Interpublic-Jardine (China) Ltd. has representative offices in Beijing, Shanghai, and Guangzhou. Its clients include Coca-Cola, Kodak, Philips, Gillette, and Heinz.

DYR Advertising Company, Ltd., a Sino-American joint venture, has acquired nine clients since it opened in 1986. They are Colgate-Palmolive, Holiday Inn, Lido Beijing, Unisys, JAL, Wartsila, Shanghai Volkswagen, Siemens, CAAC, and Beijing Stone Electronic Company, the firm's first domestic client. It expects to realize a profit in 1988.

Ogilvy & Mather's operation in China is run through two companies—one in Beijing and a specialist China Office in Hong Kong—with a total staff of about fifteen. Its Shanghai office was set up in June 1988. Currently, O & M China services about fifteen multinational clients, including General Foods, American Express, Boeing, British & American Tobacco, Nike, Parker, Philips, and Polaroid.

Grey is planning to go into China. Its biggest client in China is Bayer China with a billing around H.K. $3 million (U.S. $384,613).

Some ad agencies have chosen to locate in Hong Kong because their client base is in Hong Kong and all the decision makers are based there. JWT's aim is to establish three joint ventures in China. Clients being serviced by JWT China include McDonnell Douglas, Pepsi-Cola, Standard Chartered Bank, Lever Brothers China, R. J. Reynolds, Lufthansa, Hyatt International, International Wool Secretariat, International Business Machines, and Johnson & Johnson.

Some agencies have chosen to go into joint ventureship, a business relationship that has several advantages.

- With decisionmakers situated in China, it is easier to contact them on the spot.

- China is a big market. It is easier to collect market survey data and feedback right in China.

- Critical media contact is more constant and more convenient.

- Advertising experts are available who know the psychology and buying behaviors of the Chinese.

- Aside from multinational clients, there is always the possibility of handling some domestic clients. Leo Burnett, Singapore, has launched the latest campaign for Hangzhou Hotel in China.

While bringing profit to the joint venture itself, it will benefit the multinational clients, and at the same time upgrade the level of Chinese advertising.

Advertising Associations

There are two advertising associations in China. One is the China National Advertising Association for Foreign Economic Relations and Trade, set up in August 1981, which is the cosponsor of the Third World Advertising Congress with *South* magazine, held in Beijing from June 16–20, 1987. It has more than 100 members. The other one is China Advertising Association, set up in December 1983, with over 400 corporate members. Provincial and local advertising associations were set up in major cities. In August 1987, China Advertising Association had about fifty individual members. It has four committees: newspaper, radio, television, and advertising agencies. A technical research committee was set up in August 1987.

At the Third World Advertising Congress in Beijing (1987), with fifty-two countries in attendance, the new China Chapter of the International Advertising Association was announced.

The new IAA Chapter has thirty-two members from thirteen cities, each prominent in China's advertising industry.

> IAA members around the world will be able to increase their understanding of the Chinese market and advertising practices through contacts with members of the new chapter (Alexander Brody [speech], *IAA Airletter* No. 67, July 1987).

China International Exhibition Center (CIEC)

The China International Exhibition Center is an enterprise attached to the China Council for Promotion of International Trade.

The following CIEC exhibitions and trade fairs were scheduled for 1988: W.M. (Woodworking) Fair China '88, Machine Tools China '88, GDR Export Products, Internepcon '88, Weld Expo '88, China Print '88, China Sport '88, EP (Energy) China '88, Automotive China '88, China Textile Machinery Int'l, Int'l Packaging Technology, Metallurgical Industry Expo/China '88, Ifat '88, Mining China '88, Geology '88, Expo Comm '88, Land Transport Expo/China '88, Truck Expo '88, Asiandex '88, Preservative '88, Garmentech '88, AV & Broadcasting '88, Chemtech China '88, Industrial and Public Security '88.

The 1989 schedule includes: Oil Expo, Int'l Logimachinery Expo, Medical China, China Build, Telecomp, Aerospace, China Chem, Chinatagas, Argo Expo/China '89, Int'l Food Processing Technology Exh., Int'l Exh. on Forestry Woodworking Industries, China Instrument and Meter Exh., Fire Protech, China Heatex, Biotech, Shipbuild, Int'l Cultural & Educational Equipment Exh., Asiadex, Int'l Arts and Crafts Processing Equipment and Technology Exh., Tunneltech, Int'l System Engineering Exh. and Conference, Mining Technology Exh. and Conference, Industry Expo/China '89, Int'l Optical Fiber and Program Control Technology Exh., Int'l Tourism, Int'l Salt Processing Industry Exh., China Paper, Int'l Water Conservation and Electricity Exh., China Plastics.

From the Business Pages

World Ad Expo Aims at China

An exhibition of advertising in foreign countries, the first of its kind in China, was held from April 24–May 2, 1986 at Xuhui Cultural Center in the Xuhui District of Shanghai. It was sponsored by Xu Bai-yi, who was celebrating his fifty-five years in advertising.

The main aim of the exhibition was to upgrade the level of Chinese advertising by introducing modern advertising techniques to China. A total of 7,328 people visited the exhibition (IAA, 1987 Annual Report).

6

Advertising Media in China

Newspapers and Advertising Rates*

According to a speech made by Bao Yu Jun, Secretary General of the *People's Daily* at the Third World Advertising Congress, China has as many as 1,700 newspapers, with a total daily issue of some 202 million copies.

Papers with a daily issue of over 1 million copies include: *People's Daily, Reference News, Guangming Daily, Worker's Daily, Peasant's Daily, Economic Daily, Wen Hui Bao, Liberation Daily, Yangchen Wan Bao* (evening paper), *Xin Min Wan Bao* (evening paper), *Chinese Youth,* and *People's Liberation Army.*

People's Daily

People's Daily became the official organ of the Party Central Committee in August 1949. It is eight pages in folio and is printed in more than thirty cities. Its daily circulation is about three and a half million copies in China and abroad.

*Advertising rates mentioned in this chapter are subject to confirmation.

The current advertising rate is U.S. $105.00 per col-cm for up to eight columns, one insertion.

People's Daily Overseas Edition

The overseas edition of *People's Daily* started publication on July 1, 1985. It is eight pages in folio, published daily, and printed in Beijing, Hong Kong, Tokyo, San Francisco, and Paris, with a daily circulation of 300,000.

The advertising rate is U.S. $15.00 per col-cm for up to eight columns, one insertion.

China Daily

China Daily is the only English-language national newspaper published in the People's Republic of China, being distributed both inside China and abroad. It is read by Chinese officials, professionals, tradespeople, and students. It also reaches foreign diplomats, businesspersons, correspondents, technicians, experts, and a large number of tourists visiting China.

The advertising rates are U.S. $14.00 per col-cm, or U.S. $4,900 for full-page, $2,450 for half-page.

There is no ABC as yet in China. Circulation figures are roundabout and pass-over readers are not included. For instance, although *People's Daily* has a circulation of three and a half million, it is subscribed to by many organizations; each copy reaches quite a few people. This type of readership is significantly higher than in the United States, for example, where the newspaper is read at breakfast or in a car or subway, and is thrown away afterwards.

Trade readership is also greater in China for newspapers. Many newspapers have a specific audience. Trade newspaper titles include *Worker's Daily*, read by workers because it is subscribed to by trade unions; and *Health News*, read by physicians and public health workers.

So it is possible to select the right newspapers according to the commodity and its prospective consumers.

Sometimes special editions of newspapers can be utilized because advertisements of important organizations of a country or a city can be placed in the same issue. For instance, *China Daily* publishes special supplements from time to time. A "Supplement of Japanese Industrial and Commercial Firms" was sent free with the regular issue on September 29, 1987. Advertisements of Marubeni Corporation, the Long Term Credit Bank of Japan, Ltd., Canon, Sanwa Bank, Kumagai Gumi Group, Ismay Publications Co., New Japan Securities Co., Ltd., Fuji Bank, Nikko Securities, Okasan Securities Co., Ltd., the Hokkaido Takushoku Bank, Ltd., Hitachi Shipyard, Saitama Bank, and Daiwa Securities Co., Ltd. were inserted.

Magazines

After Liberation

Since Liberation, the number of magazines has greatly increased. In 1965, there were 790 national, provincial, and local magazines, more than 2.5 times the figure for 1950. During the "cultural revolution," most magazines were forced to cease publication.

After 1976, magazines again flourished. A total of 930 magazines were published in 1978. In two years, the figure had doubled. Over 6,000 are published today.

Magazines in China, 1980

Subject	Number of titles
General	58
Social Science	210
Natural Science and Technology	1,384
Culture and Education	179
Literature and Art	265
Juvenile	43
Pictorial	52
Total	2,191

Magazines in Shanghai, 1985

Subject	Number of titles	Average issue (10,000)
General	6	7.9
Philosophy, Social Science	88	420.9
Natural Science and Technology	276	401.6
Culture and Education	73	838.8
Literature and Art	32	1,036.1
Juvenile	13	607.9
Pictorial	3	110.8
Total	491	3,424.0

According to the figures shown in these tables, natural science and technology magazines are most numerous. They provide an effective medium for capital goods and equipment advertising.

Some of the magazines have a circulation of over one half million; *Youth Generation* claimed to have a circulation of four million, and *Culture and Life* around one million. A full-color advertisement on the back cover of the former costs U.S. $5,000 and on the latter U.S. $2,500.

Radio and Television
Radio Advertising Today

China's broadcasting consists of radio broadcasting in the cities and wired broadcasting in the countryside. At the beginning of 1979, the Central People's Broadcasting Station took the lead in offering advertising at all levels of programs.

The total turnover of nationwide broadcasting advertising in 1986 reached 38.29 million yuan, among which the turnover of radio advertising amounted to 35.64 million yuan; wire advertising accounted for a 2.65 million yuan turnover.

Research puts the private possession of radios at approximately 300 million. Radio broadcasting reaches every household. And, as in other countries, advertising rates in radio broadcasting are relatively low (sixty seconds in prime time costs U.S. $400).

TV Advertising Today

So far, China has 363 TV stations and about 81.2 million TV sets have entered Chinese households. There is a daily TV viewership of approximately 350 million. TV advertising revenue was at 115 million yuan at the end of 1986.

Most of the TV commercials range from thirty seconds to ten seconds in length, and are telecast during the intervals between programs. Generally speaking, advertisers' telecasting time does not exceed 10 percent of total telecasting hours.

Percentages of different products using TV commercials are

- Cosmetics   31.2
- Medicine   28.9
- Domestic electric appliances   23.4
- Capital goods   11.2
- Foods and drinks   3.1
- Newspapers and magazines   1.8
- Social welfare   0.4

Source: Wang Nansheng (speech), Third World Advertising Congress.

In 1979, a majority of advertisements were for Japanese commodities. From 1986, TV ads are used by American and European firms, such as Boeing, Procter & Gamble, Coca-Cola, Philips, Maxwell House, and Du Pont.

TV stations often help make commercials for local clients. The following figures show the number of TV commercials made by Shanghai TV, and reflect the growth of local TV advertising.

Year	Spots	Year	Spots
1979	123	1983	507
1980	185	1984	594
1981	198	1985	725
1982	470	1986	1,016

Advertising Rates, Central TV (U.S. $)

		15 seconds	30 seconds	60 seconds
Channel 2†	A*	2,000	4,000	6,000
	B	1,670	3,300	5,000
	C	670	1,340	2,000
Channel 8	A	670	1,340	2,000
	B	560	1,120	1,670
	C	220	440	670

*A = 7:00 P.M.–11:00 P.M. on Saturday or Sunday; B = 7:00 P.M.–11:00 P.M. from Monday to Friday; C = Daytime, Sunday to Saturday.
†Channel 2 is nationwide, with 200 million viewers. Channel 8 reaches Beijing, Tianjin, and parts of Hebei Province with a viewership of about ten million.

Advertising Rates, Shanghai TV (U.S. $)*

15 seconds	30 seconds	60 seconds
550	1,100	2,200

*Shanghai's reach approaches eighty million daily, out of a surrounding population of approximately 230 million.

Radio and TV Publications

Shanghai Broadcasting and TV Weekly is an eight-page tabloid equivalent to *TV Guide*, with a weekly circulation of two million. The advertising rate for 130 sq. cm. is 3,150 RMB (U.S. $870).

Shanghai Television is a monthly published by Shanghai TV with a circulation of 300,000. The advertising rates in U.S. are $3,000 for full-page 4/c back cover; $2,000 for full-page 4/c inside front cover; $1,000 for full-page, B/W.

CBC has made an arrangement with Central TV to exchange TV shows for TV commercial time. Advertisers on Central TV now include Du Pont, Boeing, Kodak, and Philips.

Outdoor Advertising

Outdoor advertising in China has a quite long history. It is still an effective advertising medium today.

Billboards

Shanghai has a total of about 800 billboards of different sizes (7,000 billboards are set up nationwide). Besides domestic merchandise, Japanese commodities and other foreign companies are using billboard advertising. Advertisers include United Airlines, Northwest Airlines, Singapore Airlines, and Telefunken. The rate of billboard advertising varies according to size and location. Rates are approximately U.S. $30.00/sq.m/mo.

Neon Signs

Neon signage is not only an effective advertising medium, it is also judged to enhance a city's looks. The advertising rate depends on the cost of mounting and rental.

Transit Advertising

Some cities like Shanghai have advertising on the sides of buses and trolleys. Such advertisements, 750cm high and 5.2 m–5.7 m long, on three lines, cost U.S. $7,000 for six months.

Light Boxes

Many shops use light boxes as shop signs. This device has become quite popular for advertising outside or inside stores, and it, too, is judged to enhance its surroundings. Best results are had with accompanying literature handouts. The price varies according to the size and materials used.

Window Displays

Sony now occupies China's premier window display location—the east side corner of Shanghai's No. 1 Department Store. When the

store was under construction in the 1930s, the far-sighted proprietor made certain that no entrance took up valuable window space
on the building's corners.

Direct Mail

Direct mail has little competition in China, and so receives good
response from prospects.

Mailing lists can be compiled from all kinds of directories in
China. Many are published in English, while some provinces like
Jiangsu, Jiangxi, and Yunnan have separate volumes in Chinese.
Every larger city has telephone books with addresses.

Moreover, although advertising material can be mailed only according to the price of mailing letters, the postage required is still
lower than in foreign countries. There are two regular postage
rates:

- outport (the equivalent of USPS first class) $.022 per ounce

- local (within provinces) .011 per ounce

Generally, foreign companies mail in bulk, with an agent in China authorized to address the envelope and do the mailing.

Exhibitions and Mini Sales
Exhibitions

The China Council for the Promotion of International Trade, with
its head office in Beijing, and sub-councils in many provinces, has
an International Exhibition Center in Beijing and a center for
recommending catalogs and samples of foreign commodities.

Adsale in Hong Kong can arrange exhibitions to be held in China. China International Advertising Corporation can also arrange
exhibitions of different scales. Shanghai Advertising Corporation
has a special exhibition department, as mentioned.

The Shanghai No. 1 Department Store has an Exposition Hall on
its fifth floor.

Mini fairs can be held in department stores. For instance,
Shanghai No. 2 Department Store regularly holds mini exhibitions

of imported cosmetics and perfumes. Featured products are often from France, Italy, United States, and Switzerland, with prices ranging from approximately U.S. $.25–45.00.

The Shanghai No. 1 Department Store has a special counter selling French perfumes. Perfumes priced at the equivalent of U.S. $10.00 are most salable.

Promotions

When Nescafe and Maxwell House Instant entered Shanghai and Guangzhou, they both ran big sample promotion campaigns.

Tang, a famous American brand, markets its instant orange juice drink in China. The product itself is manufactured by Sino-American Tianmei Food Co., Ltd., Tianjin, under license from General Foods Corporation, N.Y., U.S.A. When Tang entered the Shanghai market, besides advertising in newspapers and over the TV station, free cups of Tang were given out at food stores. Sales increased a great deal although a 500-gram bottle is sold at a "pricey" (at that time) 8.70 yuan (U.S. $2.40).

Sponsorship is another successful form of PR. Sporting events are most frequently sponsored, and result in effective promotion of brand-awareness.

Media Reach Surveys

Beijing

The Society of Journalism, Beijing, Journalism Research Institute of China Social Science Academy made a survey by sending out 2,430 questionnaires to find a way of improving and reforming newspapers and radio and TV broadcasting. Two thousand four hundred and twenty-three questionnaires were received. The survey was conducted from June 8 to August 6, 1982. The respondents, residents over thirteen years old, provided a sample size of nearly 7,000. Some of the results follow:

Audience, by Age (%)

Category	13–17	18–25	26–35	36–60	60+
Radio listener	98.9	98.7	96.1	96.3	94.4
TV viewer	96.2	96.2	92.3	90.2	86.5
Newspaper reader	86.0	86.4	82.4	79.1	62.7

Audience, by Education (%)

Category	Semiliterate	Levels of education		
		Primary school	Secondary school	College
Radio listener	92.9	93.4	98.4	99.0
TV viewer	72.9	86.4	95.5	95.8
Newspaper reader	40.0	62.7	89.6	99.9

Interest in Radio Commercials

	(%)
By sex:	
Male (1338 persons)	3.0
Female (990 persons)	2.5
By resident:	
Urban (1682 persons)	2.3
Rural (646 persons)	4.2
By vocation:	
Worker (712 persons)	3.2
Peasant (608 persons)	4.3

Interest in TV Commercials

By sex:	(%)
Male (1284 persons)	1.1
Female (954 persons)	1.2
By resident:	
Urban (1648 persons)	0.7
Rural (590 persons)	2.4
By vocation:	
Worker (703 persons)	0.7
Peasant (553 persons)	2.5

Interest in Newspaper Ads

By sex:	(%)
Male (1125 persons)	2.2
Female (769 persons)	2.3
By resident:	
Urban (1662 persons)	1.5
Rural (272 persons)	7.0
By vocation:	
Worker (684 persons)	2.3
Peasant (239 persons)	7.5

Source: *China News Yearbook*, 1983.

Zhejiang Province

Another survey was conducted by sample in Zhejiang Province from the middle of September to the middle of November 1983. Questionnaires and personal interviews were used. Out of 2,598 questionnaires, there was a 97.5 percent reply.

Generally speaking, in Zhejiang Province, among respondents over the age of twelve, 67.3 percent read newspapers, 96.5 percent listen to radio broadcasting, and 75.1 percent view TV. Of these, 59.8 percent did all three on a regular basis.

The earlier-mentioned figures showed that the percentage of radio broadcasting was the highest, because the reach of radio is more or less the same in city and rural population, whereas the newspaper readership differs between the two populations.

Advertising Reach, by Vocation (%)

Vocational	Newspaper		Radio broadcast*		TV	
1. City workers†	(665)	5.3	(754)	16.8	(725)	1.8
2. Rural workers	(366)	11.7	(713)	17.5	(443)	6.5
3. Commercial & service	(135)	4.4	(151)	19.2	(143)	2.1
4. Veterans	(118)	3.4	(120)	9.2	(117)	0.9
5. Financial management	(116)	3.4	(120)	8.3	(117)	1.7
6. Technicians	(77)	2.6	(78)	12.8	(76)	1.3
7. Teaching, public health, sport	(157)	3.2	(159)	4.4	(153)	0.7
8. Students	(266)	4.9	(273)	15.8	(250)	2.8
9. Retired	(64)	–	(114)	10.5	(100)	–
10. Waiting to be employed	(16)	6.3	(18)	22.2	(18)	–
11. Individual operators	(18)	5.6	(27)	25.9	(26)	–
12. Others	(5)	20.0	(5)	40.0	(5)	–
13. Urban	(1430)	4.0	(1590)	13.8	(1522)	1.3
14. Rural	(573)	10.1	(942)	17.8	(651)	5.7

Source: *China News Yearbook* 1984.
*Based on listeners to the most broadly based program.
†Sample size.

The figures indicate greatest interest in media advertising from the rural population. This shows the active growth of that group as a consumer market, as encouraged by a significant rise in country-side living standards.

Henan Province

Another survey made in Henan Province among 805 people of different ages showed that 58 percent watch TV every day, 25 percent watch TV more than three times a week, and only 2 percent of them do not watch TV programs. Eighty-four percent of those watching think too many TV commercials would waste their time.

Favorite TV commercials featured products or services of Boeing, DuPont, Lux, Camay, and Coca-Cola (*Economic Daily*, November 1, 1987).

From the Business Pages

TV News

China has become the third largest maker of TV sets in the world, behind the United States and Japan, with its annual output reaching an estimated sixteen million sets in 1987, including six million color TV sets.

The whole country has 23 large TV factories, each turning out more than 200,000 sets a year. Factories have been built in Shanghai, Jiangsu, Tianjin, Beijing, Sichuan, Shaanxi, Guangdong, and Fujian.

Because of imported foreign technology and equipment and the localization of component production, China's TV industry has been developing rapidly and has attracted the world's attention. More than 10 factories have sold their sets to Southeast Asia, Europe, North America, and other parts of the world. Between 1978 and 1986, the country produced 68.96 million TV sets, with 12 billion yuan profit paid to the State (*China Daily*, November 28, 1987).

Advertising Revenue

The 1987 advertising revenue of Central TV Station is expected to reach 20 million yuan. After October 26, 1987, each daily news program will be followed by 60 seconds devoted to public service advertising (*China Features* No. 6, p. 1).

Central TV Surveys asked the Public Opinion Institute of People's University to make a survey in Beijing and Tianjin in July 1987. From 1,200 samples, 68.3% preferred TV advertising; 31% preferred press, radio broadcasting, and billboard advertising; 41% claimed that there are too many TV commercials. Of these, 66.4% preferred domestic advertising and 33.6% preferred foreign commercials. The most impressive foreign commercials advertised include Hitachi, Toshiba, Kodak, and Coca-Cola (*China Features*, No. 6, p. 12).

7

Guidelines for Advertising in China

The Local Touch

In the United States, many people are advocating "global" marketing. The title of New York-based Grey Advertising, Inc.'s, booklet *Global Vision with Local Touch* more realistically defines this approach. Again, although in general, western techniques are applicable to advertising in China, and are helpful in upgrading the level of Chinese advertising, cultural differences must never be undervalued.

Consider, for example, identity and trademark appeal. One Chinese battery company carelessly applied their "white elephant" trademark to their export products. Now in China, the elephant is well liked because it symbolizes the "fresh start of a new year." But in western countries a "white elephant" is something useless. That company's failure to sell batteries abroad may have been averted with a little research.

Similarly, well-known Western trademarks, such as the snake-entwined caduceus on medical items, and the wise owl in publishers' identities, may have to be abandoned for the Chinese market. Snakes and owls do not hold much favor with the Chinese. Though snake soup, for example, is a featured culinary item in Guangdong Province, to taste it is still considered daring.

Recently an advertising lecturer came to Shanghai with a TV commercial he had designed for Ivory Soap. In it a Chinese family—father, mother, and children—all go to the paddy field to transplant rice shoots. Later, they emerge covered with soil, and use Ivory Soap to clean up. This TV commercial was completely off the mark. For one thing, this particular task is now done by machine. But—and this is most important—no one who is experienced in this work becomes so soiled. The image of dirtiness, which may be used with some appeal abroad, is simply insulting to the Chinese working consumer. Evidently the commercial was made with a minimum of research. "Ivory—the soap that floats," is still the best approach in China.

Foreign Label Impact
Market Survey for Philips International

In April 1986, Walmsley Ltd. prepared for Philips International "An Evaluation of the Philips TV and Print Advertising Campaign in China," a document that summarized ". . . the results of a series of group discussions conducted in Beijing on April 5–7, 1986, designed to evaluate consumer reaction to Philips corporate and color television advertising campaign in China." A similar focus group had been assembled earlier in Shanghai. The findings are excerpted below.

Reactions to TV commercials.

1. Corporate Advertisement: As in Shanghai, this ad was considered too fast to follow, while the range of products being shown was difficult to associate with their own lifestyles.

2. Color Television Advertisement: This ad was better received because it involves a single product and one which is easily related to their own lifestyles. The ad conveyed the idea that Philip's television can provide natural, clear color.

   The groups also pointed out that Philips advertises two sizes of television: 20-inch and 14-inch. In their view the best size is 18-inch: the 14-inch size is considered too small, while the 20-inch size is too big.

3. Corporate Advertisement (animated): As in Beijing, this ad received a more positive response than the other one because it is slower and shows products one at a time. Group members found it easier to recall the content of this ad; in particular, they were able to recall that Philips provides a repair service.

Reactions to the Print Ads.   Reactions to the print ads were quite similar to those expressed in the Shanghai groups: taken together, the print ads were considered more effective than the television ads in communicating corporate images. As in Shanghai, there was a general feeling that the Philips logo is too small and does not make good use of available space.

Reactions to the Philips Name and Logo.   As in Shanghai, all groups felt that the English and Chinese versions of the Philips name should be shown together. All agreed, however, that on the products themselves the English name and logo alone should be shown. They felt the use of Chinese characters would give the products a local flavor and, consequently in this case, a lower quality image.

The group members of the Walmsley study for Philips preferred slower ads. They also preferred ads that featured a single product easily identifiable with their lifestyles. Perhaps more significantly, their suggestion to increase the size of Philips' logo indicated the strong appeal of the company identity. In China, as in most countries, there is a specific range of products for which the foreign label demonstrates a positive consumer impact.

Brand Distinction

The Chinese idiom "Say what everybody says" no longer applies to advertising. Though counter-advertising has not yet entered the media, advertisers in China must find a way to let consumers know what makes their products and services different. Years ago, the Monkey King (from the novel, *A Trip to the West*) was used to advertise a successful Japanese commodity on a billboard in Beijing. Afterwards, many other advertisers also used the Monkey King, prompting a French advertising expert to comment, "If everybody uses Monkey King, he will be too busy."

More recently, clerks in a small shop on Sin Hua Road in Shanghai were mislabeling bars of Camay soap *li shi xiang zao* (Lux Beauty Soap). The packaging of the leading brands in China's crowded imported soap market is quite similar. The wrappers of Lux, "the beauty soap of international film stars," and Camay, "the soap of beautiful women," and two other leading brands all feature portraits of glamorous foreign women.

The following headlines, taken from advertisements in *China Daily,* show how advertisers in the highly competitive airline and banking industries have managed to distinguish themselves—without comparative advertising.

Airlines
Three ways to make your vacation dollar fly further (Northwest)

Cathay Pacific. Purrrrrrfection (Cathay Pacific)

The cheapest way to fly to London (British)

New flight schedule, the same friendly service (All Nippon Airways)

Our high standards aren't reflected in our fares (Lufthansa)

With Pakistan International Airlines it's just like coming home (PIA)

Aeroflot is at your service! (Aeroflot, Soviet Airlines)

There's a newer, faster way to travel to beautiful Poland (Polish Airlines)

Banks
Putting together a business deal in China can sometimes be a bit puzzling (Bank of America)

We have a lot of experience of trade financing with China. It's yours for the asking now in Beijing (Royal Bank of Canada)

An Italian bank to be found the world over (Banca Nazionale del Lavoro)

Time is money   Trust is gold   In Beijing too (Cariplo)

Your new far east connection Deutsche Bank in Beijing (Deutsche Bank)

National Bank of Pakistan comes to Beijing (National Bank of Pakistan)

Series Advertising

Given the focus groups' preference for slower, single-product ads, it is advisable to design a series of advertisements. For instance, Isuzu of Japan ran a series of advertisements that included the headlines *Isuzu cars running on the Tibet Plateau* and *Can transport Chinese cabbage as well as cement* to demonstrate the ruggedness and versatility of its automobiles. And a series of advertisements from Toshiba of Japan aroused interest in Toshiba's line of products by introducing readers to Japanese traditions.

Informative Advertising

Informative advertisements create goodwill among consumers. Sony ran a series of twenty-six advertisements consisting of advice, such as "Don't put a flower vase on the top of your TV set," and "Don't oil the tape player yourself," accompanied by explanations. Based on the success of this first batch of advertisements, a second batch followed, covering such topics as "Why color TV has color" and where to go for Sony spare parts.

In 1987, Toshiba gave advice on "the proper and effective use of refrigerators" through a series of half-page ads.

Advertisers will find that there are not many competent copy-writers in China. In addition, they will discover that the language barrier often obstructs the appeal of a message more effectively than it does the meaning. Fortunately, Chinese is rich in idioms that have a useful appeal in advertising.

A Chinese shoe factory successfully adopted the words of the ancient philosopher Lao Zi "A thousand-li journey starts with the first step."

Chinese-made Kaige TV sets used the common saying "It is far away beyond the horizon, yet as near as a few feet" accompanied by the image of a sporting event telecast from Spain. Ricoh used a similar catch phrase for its facsimile transmitter.

A Japanese advertisement suggesting the use of Sakura color film with Konica cameras adopted the Chinese idiom "Add flowers to embroidery." Because Sakura is a kind of flower (called "ying hua" in Chinese), this idiom is quite suitable.

A Mitsubishi billboard advertisement read "When friends come from afar, please ride in a Mitsubishi car." This is derived from Confucius's saying, "When friends come from afar, how joyful it is!"

For its line of ladies' watches, Citizen used, "Elegant on the out-side and clever in the inside," complimenting both the watch and its wearer.

The adage "unwilling to give up even a hair" normally implies stinginess. But when applied to a toothbrush, as it was in a memorable pre-Liberation advertisement, it means that the bristles will not fall out.

Some Dos and Don'ts

Dos:

1. Do get familiar with the various governmental regulations.*

   - Advertisements for pharmaceuticals and cosmetics must be approved by the Public Health Bureau.

   - Sales promotion giveaways like T-shirts are regulated by the Bureau of Industry and Commerce Administration.

   - Cigarette advertisements are banned on radio and television and in publications.

   - Liquor advertising is strictly controlled.

   - TV commercials can be placed only before and after the program.

2. Do insist upon a competent translator.

3. Do be careful if a map is to be used in an ad.

4. Do be convenient for the viewer, listener, or reader to contact.

Don'ts:

1. Don't say you are "the leader."

2. Don't put your ad on the back of envelopes. Starting July 1, 1987, the Chinese Post Office began to reject mail with advertising on the back of the envelope.

3. Don't use sex appeal.

---

*See Appendixes of this book for summaries of China's Trademark Law and Regulations for Advertising Management.

A Fresh Start for Advertising in China

Advertising in China is both old and new. It is old because advertising in China has a very long and proven history of success. It is new because advertising only reappeared in the spring of 1979, merely a decade ago. The opportunity to have a fresh impact today through advertising cannot be ignored.

Appendix I

Trademark Law of the People's Republic of China*

Chapter I General Provisions

Article 1. This Law is enacted for the purposes of improving the administration of trademarks, of protecting the exclusive right to use a trademark, and of encouraging producers to guarantee the quality of their goods and maintain the reputation of their trademarks, with a view to protecting consumer interests and to promoting the development of socialist commodity economy.

Article 2. The Trademark Office of the administrative authority for industry and commerce under the State Council shall be responsible for the registration and administrative control of trademarks throughout the country.

*Adopted at the Twenty-Fourth Session of the Standing Committee of the Fifth National People's Congress, on August 23, 1982.

Article 3. Registered trademark means a trademark which has been approved and registered by the Trademark Office. The trademark registrant shall enjoy an exclusive right to use the trademark, which right shall be protected by law.

Article 4. Any enterprise, institution, or individual producer or trader, intending to acquire the exclusive right to use a trademark for the goods produced, manufactured, processed, selected, or marketed by it or him, shall file an application for the registration of the trademark with the Trademark Office.

Article 5. Where the State prescribes that certain kinds of goods must bear a registered trademark, registration of a trademark must be applied for in respect of such goods. Where no trademark registration has been granted, such goods shall not be sold in the market.

Article 6. Any user of a trademark shall be responsible for the quality of the goods in respect of which the trademark is used. The administrative authorities for industry and commerce at all levels shall, through the administrative control of trademarks, exercise supervision over the quality of the goods and shall stop any practice that deceives consumers.

Article 7. Any word, design, or their combination, used as a trademark, must be distinctive so that it be distinguishable. Where a registered trademark is used, it should carry the indication "Registered Trademark" or a sign indicating that it is registered.

Article 8. In trademarks, the following words or designs shall not be used:

1. Those identical with or similar to the State name, national flag, national emblem, military flag, or decorations, of the People's Republic of China;

2. Those identical with or similar to the State names, national flags, national emblems, or military flags, of foreign countries;

3. Those identical with or similar to the flags, emblems or names, of international intergovernmental organizations;

4. Those identical with or similar to the symbols, or names, of the Red Cross or the Red Crescent;

5. Those relating to generic names or designs of the goods in respect of which the trademark is used;

6. Those having direct reference to the quality, main raw materials, function, use, weight, quantity, or other features of the goods in respect of which the trademark is used;

7. Those having the nature of discrimination against any nationality;

8. Those having the nature of exaggeration and deceit in advertising goods;

9. Those detrimental to socialist morals or customs, or having other unhealthy influences.

Article 9.   Any foreigner or foreign enterprise intending to apply for the registration of a trademark in China shall file an application in accordance with any agreement concluded between the People's Republic of China and the country to which the applicant belongs, or according to the international treaty to which both countries are parties, or on the basis of the principle of reciprocity.

Article 10.   Any foreigner or foreign enterprise intending to apply for the registration of a trademark, or to deal with other matters concerning a trademark in China, shall entrust the organization designated by the State to act on his or its behalf.

Chapter II   Application for Trademark Registration

Article 11.   Any application for the registration of a trademark shall, in a form, indicate, in accordance with the prescribed classification of goods, the class of the goods and the designation of the goods in respect of which the trademark is intended to be used.

Article 12.   Where any applicant intends to use the same trademark for goods in different classes, a separate application for registration shall be filed in respect of each class of the prescribed classification of goods.

Article 13. Where a registered trademark is intended to be used in respect of other goods of the same class, a new application for registration shall be filed.

Article 14. Where any word and/or design of a registered trademark is to be altered, a new registration shall be applied for.

Article 15. Where, after the registration of a trademark, the name, address, or other registered matters concerning the registrant change, an application regarding the change shall be filed.

Chapter III Examination for, and Approval of, Trademark Registration

Article 16. Where the trademark for which registration has been applied for is in conformity with the relevant provisions of this Law, the Trademark Office shall, after examination, preliminarily approve the trademark and publish it.

Article 17. Where the trademark for which registration has been applied for is not in conformity with the relevant provisions of this Law, or where it is identical with or similar to the trademark of another person which, in respect of the same or similar goods, has been registered or, after examination, preliminarily approved, the Trademark Office shall refuse the application and shall not publish the said trademark.

Article 18. Where two or more applicants apply for the registration of identical or similar trademarks for the same or similar goods, the preliminary approval, after examination, and the publication shall be made for the trademark which was first filed. Where applications are filed on the same day, the preliminary approval, after examination, and the publication shall be made for the trademark which was the earliest used, and the applications of the others shall be refused and their trademarks shall not be published.

Article 19. Any person may, within three months from the date of the publication, file an opposition against the trademark which, after examination, has been preliminarily approved. If no opposition is filed, or if it is decided that the opposition is not justified, registration shall be approved, a trademark registration certificate shall be issued, and the trademark shall be published. If it is decided that the oppositon is justified, no registration shall be approved.

Article 20.   The Trademark Review and Adjudication Board, established under the administrative authority for industry and commerce under the State Council, shall be responsible for handling trademark disputes.

Article 21.   Where the application for registration of a trademark is refused and no publication of the trademark is made, the Trademark Office shall notify the applicant in writing. Where the applicant is dissatisfied, he may, within fifteen days from the receipt of the notification, apply for a review. The Trademark Review and Adjudication Board shall make a final decision and notify the applicant in writing.

Article 22.   Where an opposition is filed against the trademark which, after examination, has been preliminarily approved and published, the Trademark Office shall hear the opponent and the applicant state facts and grounds and shall, after investigation and verification, make a decision. Where any party is dissatisfied, it may, within fifteen days from the receipt of the notification, apply for review, and the Trademark Review and Adjudication Board shall make a final decision, and notify the opponent and the applicant in writing.

Chapter IV   Renewal, Assignment, and Licensing of Registered Trademarks

Article 23.   The period of validity of a registered trademark shall be ten years counted from the date of the approval of the registration.

Article 24.   Where the registrant intends to continue to use the registered trademark beyond the expiration of the period of validity, an application for renewal of the registration shall be made within six months before the said expiration. Where no such application could be filed within the said period, an extension period of six months may be allowed. If no application is filed by the expiration of the extension period, the registered trademark shall be canceled.

The period of validity of each renewal of registration shall be ten years.

Any renewal of registration shall be published after approval.

Article 25.   Where a registered trademark is assigned, the assignor and assignee shall jointly file an application with the Trademark Office. The assignee shall guarantee the quality of the goods in respect of which the registered trademark is used.

The assignment of the registered trademark shall be published after approval.

Article 26.   Any trademark registrant may, by signing a trademark license contract, authorize other persons to use his registered trademark. The licensor shall supervise the quality of the goods in respect of which the licensee uses his registered trademark, and the licensee shall guarantee the quality of the goods in respect of which the registered trademark is used.

The trademark license contract shall be submitted to the Trademark Office for the file.

Chapter V   Adjudication of Disputes concerning Registered Trademarks

Article 27.   Any person disputing a registered trademark may, within one year from the date of approval of the trademark registration, apply to the Trademark Review and Adjudication Board for adjudication.

The Trademark Review and Adjudication Board shall, after the receipt of the application for adjudication, notify the interested parties and request them to respond with arguments within a specified period.

Article 28.   Where the trademark, before being approved for registration, has been the object of opposition and decision, no application for adjudication, based on the same facts and grounds, may be made.

Article 29.   After the Trademark Review and Adjudication Board has made the final decision maintaining or cancelling the disputed registered trademark, it shall notify the interested parties in writing.

Chapter VI   Administrative Control of the Use of Trademarks

Article 30.   Where any person who uses the registered trademark commits any of the following, the Trademark Office shall order him to rectify the situation within a specified period or shall cancel the registered trademark:

1. Where any word, design, or their combination of the registered trademark is altered unilaterally (that is, without the required registration);

2. Where the name, address, or other registered matters concerning the registrant of a registered trademark are changed unilaterally (that is, without the required application);

3. Where the registered trademark is assigned unilaterally (that is, without the required approval);

4. Where the registered trademark has ceased to be used for three consecutive years.

Article 31.   Where the registered trademark is used in respect of goods which have been roughly or poorly manufactured, or whose superior quality has been replaced by inferior quality, (so that) consumers are deceived, the administrative authorities for industry and commerce at all levels shall, according to the circumstances, order the rectification of the situation within a specified period, and may, in addition, circulate a notice of criticism or impose a fine, or the Trademark Office may cancel the registered trademark.

Article 32. Where the registered trademark is canceled or has expired and not been renewed, the Trademark Office shall not approve, during one year from the date of the cancellation or the removal on account of expiration, applications for registration of trademarks identical with or similar to the said trademark.

Article 33. In the case of any person violating the provisions of Article 5 of this Law, the local administrative authorities for industry and commerce shall order him to file an application for registration within a specified period, and may, in addition, impose a fine.

Article 34. Where any person who uses an unregistered trademark commits any of the following, the local administrative authorities for industry and commerce shall stop the use of the trademark, order him to rectify the situation within a specified period, and may, in addition, circulate a notice of criticism or impose a fine:

1. Where the trademark is falsely represented as registered;

2. Where any provision of Article 8 of this Law is violated;

3. Where the manufacture is rough or poor, or where superior quality is replaced by inferior quality, (so that) consumers are deceived.

Article 35. Any party, dissatisfied with the decision of the Trademark Office to cancel the registered trademark, may apply for review within fifteen days from the receipt of the corresponding notice. The Trademark Review and Adjudication Board shall make a final decision and notify the applicant in writing.

Article 36. Any party dissatisfied with the decision of an administrative authority for industry and commerce imposing a fine under the provisions of Article 31, Article 33, or Article 34 may institute proceedings with the people's court within fifteen days from the receipt of the corresponding notice. If no proceedings are instituted or if there is no performance complying with the decision imposing the fine by the expiration of the said period, the administrative authority for industry and commerce concerned may ask the people's court for compulsory execution.

Chapter VII   Protection of the Exclusive Right to Use Registered Trademarks

Article 37.   The exclusive right to use a registered trademark is limited to the trademark which has been approved for registration and to the goods in respect of which the use of the trademark has been approved.

Article 38.   Any of the following acts shall be an infringement of the exclusive right to use a registered trademark:

1. To use a trademark which is identical with or similar to the registered trademark in respect of the same or similar goods without the authorization of the proprietor of the registered trademark;

2. To make or sell, without authorization, representations of the registered trademark of another person;

3. To cause, in other respects, prejudice to the exclusive right to use the registered trademark of another person.

Article 39.   In the case of any of the acts infringing the exclusive right to use a registered trademark as provided for in Article 38 of this Law, the party whose right was infringed may request the administrative authority for industry and commerce, at or above the county level, of the location (domicile or establishment) of the infringer to handle (the matter). The administrative authority for industry and commerce concerned shall have the power to order the infringer to stop the infringing act immediately and to compensate the party whose right was infringed for the damages suffered. The amount of compensation shall be the profit which the infringer has earned through the infringement during the period of the infringement or the damages that the party whose right was infringed has suffered through the infringement during the period of the infringement. If the circumstances are serious, the said authority may, in addition, impose a fine. Any dissatisfied party may institute proceedings with the people's court within fifteen days from the receipt of the notice. If no proceedings are instituted or if there is no performance complying with the decision imposing the fine by the expiration of the said period, the administrative authority for industry and commerce concerned may ask the people's court for compulsory execution.

Where the exclusive right to use the registered trademark was infringed, the party whose right was infringed may institute proceedings directly with the people's court.

Article 40. Any party that passes off a registered trademark of another person—including any party that makes or sells, without authorization, representations of the registered trademark of another person—shall compensate for the damages suffered by the party whose right was infringed and additionally shall be imposed a ermore, any person directly responsible for the passing off shall be prosecuted, according to law, by the judicial organs in respect of criminal responsibility.

Chapter VIII Supplementary Provisions

Article 41. Any application for trademark registration and any other proceeding in trademark matters shall be subject to the payment of a fee. The rate of the fees shall be prescribed separately.

Article 42. The Implementing Regulations of this Law shall be drawn up by the administrative authority for industry and commerce under the State Council. They shall enter into force after they have been submitted to and approved by the State Council.

Article 43. This Law shall enter into force on March 1, 1983. The "Regulations Governing Trademarks" promulgated by the State Council on April 10, 1963, shall be abrogated on the same date, and any other provisions concerning trademarks contrary to this Law shall cease to be effective at the same time.

Trademarks registered before this Law enters into force shall continue to be valid.

Appendix II

Regulations for Advertising Management*

Article 1. These Regulations are formulated for the purposes of strengthening advertising management, promoting the development of advertising business, and effectively using advertising for the promotion of socialist construction.

Article 2. These Regulations are applicable to advertising by means of such media as newspapers, broadcasting, television, films, billboards, shop windows, printed matter, and neon lights in the People's Republic of China.

Article 3. Advertisements must be truthful, healthy, and clear in content. They are not allowed to deceive end-users and consumers in any form.

---

*Following is the full text of the new regulations for advertising management in China released by the State Council on October 26, 1987, and effective December 1, 1987.

Article 4. Monopoly and unjust competition are prohibited in advertising activities.

Article 5. Administrations for industry and commerce at state and local levels are responsible for advertising management.

Article 6. According to stipulations of these Regulations and other related decrees and regulations, organizations and self-employed individuals engaged in advertising must apply to the administrations for industry and commerce for registration based on their respective conditions:

1. Enterprises specializing in advertising businesses are issued a *Business License for Enterprise Legal Person;*

2. Institutions concurrently engaged in advertising are issued a *License for a Full Status Legal Advertising Business;*

3. Self-employed individuals capable of running an advertising business are issued a *Business License;*

4. Enterprises concurrently engaged in advertising must apply for registration of change of business range.

Article 7. The content of advertisements requested by clients shall be within the clients' business range or the range permitted by the state.

Article 8. An advertisement shall not be released if it:

1. Violates state laws or regulations;

2. Demeans the dignity of the Chinese nation;

3. Bears the symbols of China's national flag, emblem, or anthem, or is accompanied by the tune of China's national anthem;

4. Is reactionary, obscene, superstitious, or absurd in content;

5. Resorts to deception;

6. Belittles other products of the same kind.

Article 9. News media should put distinctive advertisement symbols on the advertisements they carry and shall not release advertisements in the form of news reports and get payments thereby;

news reporters are not allowed to solicit advertisements in the name of conducting interviews.

Article 10. Advertisements for cigarettes are forbidden on broadcasting, television, and newspapers. Famous and high-quality liquors which have been awarded national, ministerial, or provincial prizes can be advertised with the permission of the administrations for industry and commerce.

Article 11. Relevant certificates are needed in applications for advertising of the following:

1. For an advertisement showing the product's quality standard, the advertiser shall provide a certificate issued by a standardization management department above the provincial or municipal level, or one issued by an authorized quality-examination institution;

2. For an advertisement showing awards, the advertiser shall provide the award certificate of the most recent contest or the current year, or award certificates of past contests or years. The advertisement shall indicate the rank of the award and the issuing department.

3. For an advertisement showing quality title of the advertised product, the advertiser shall provide relevant certificates issued by the government and shall indicate in the advertisement which institution was awarded the title and when;

4. For an advertisement showing patent right, the advertiser shall provide the patent certificate;

5. For an advertisement showing a registered trademark, the advertiser shall provide the trademark registry certificate;

6. For the advertising of a product made with a production license, the advertiser shall provide the license;

7. For advertisements relating to culture, education, or health, advertisers shall provide references from their higher authorities;

8. For other advertisements which need references, advertisers must provide references from related governmental departments or from other authorized bodies.

Article 12.   Advertising executors or agents must check the content of advertisements and related certificates. Advertisements violating the rules of these Regulations shall not be released.

Article 13.   Outdoor advertisements should be put up or installed according to plans made by the administration for industry and commerce and the departments of urban construction, environmental protection, and public security under the auspices of the local government. The administration for industry and commerce shall supervise the implementation of related regulations.

No advertisement shall be put up or installed in construction-controlled areas around governmental institutions or protected cultural relics and in areas where advertisements are prohibited by the government.

Article 14.   The advertising rate is decided by those engaged in advertising business and shall be submitted to the local administration for industry and commerce for the record.

Article 15.   The commission rate for the advertising agent shall be decided jointly by the State Administration for Industry and Commerce and the state price control department.

The charge rate for the occupation of space for outdoor advertising shall be decided through consultations among the local administration for industry and commerce and the departments of price control and urban construction, and shall be submitted to the local government for approval.

Article 16.   Those engaged in advertising business must, in accordance with relevant state regulations, establish an advertisement account book, pay taxes, and accept supervision and examination by the finance and auditing departments and the administration for industry and commerce.

Article 17.   Advertising executors or agents should sign written contracts with clients which clearly lay down the responsibilities of both parties.

Article 18.   Advertisers or advertising agents, if they violate these Regulations, shall be punished in the following ways by the administration for industry and commerce according to the seriousness of their offense:

1. Ordered to stop releasing advertisements;

2. Ordered to make open corrections;

3. Criticized in a circular notice;

4. Have illegal income confiscated;

5. Get fined;

6. Ordered to wind up business for rectification;

7. Have their business license revoked.

If an offense is serious enough to constitute a crime, it shall be dealt with by judicial organs.

Article 19. Advertisers or advertising agents who do not accept the penalty decision by the administration for industry and commerce can apply for reconsideration to the administration of a higher level within fifteen days after receiving the notice of penalty. Those who still do not accept the reconsidered decision can file a suit to the People's Court within thirty days after receiving the reconsidered decision.

Article 20. Advertisers or advertising agents who have violated these Regulations and caused losses to the end-users and consumers or are guilty of other infringements on other's interests shall be responsible for compensation.

Victims can ask for compensations at the administration for industry and commerce above the county level. Advertisers or advertising agents who do not accept the arbitration of the administrations for industry and commerce can file a suit to the People's Court. Victims can also file suits directly to the People's Court.

Article 21. The State Administration for Industry and Commerce is responsible for the explanation of these Regulations and for working out detailed rules for their implementation.

Article 22. These Regulations enter into force on December 1, 1987; simultaneously, the *Interim Regulations for Advertising Management* promulgated by the State Council on February 6, 1982, are abolished.

Appendix III

Detailed Rules of Regulations for Advertising Management*

Article 1. Based on Article 21 of Regulations for Advertising Management (hereinafter referred to as "RAM"), these detailed rules are formulated.

Article 2. According to the stipulations of Article 2 of RAM, the scope of advertising control includes:

1. Advertisements placed in newspapers, periodicals, publications, directories, etc.

2. Advertisements broadcasted and shown through radio, TV, movies, video tapes, slides, etc.

3. Advertisements placed on billboards, neon signs, electronic boards, in windows, light boxes, on wall spaces, etc., erected

---

*Promulgated by State Administration of Industry and Commerce on January 9, 1988. This is a translation for reference. The Chinese version is the official document.

on constructions or in spaces of streets, squares, airports, stations, docks, etc.

4. Advertisements placed or posted inside or outside of cinemas, theaters, stadiums (gymnasiums), cultural centers, exhibition centers, guest houses, restaurants, amusement houses, markets, etc.

5. Advertisements placed, drawn and posted in/on means of traffic include cars, ships, airplanes, etc.

6. Various kinds of advertising materials mailed through the post office.

7. Advertise through giving away of presents or articles.

8. Advertising through other media or forms to publish, broadcast, erect, or post advertisements.

Article 3.   Enterprises which apply to run advertising business must conform with the following conditions, besides the conditions to register as an enterprise:

1. Having specialized market research organization with professional personnel;

2. Having managing personnel who are familiar with the RAM and designers, production personnel, and copy editor;

3. Having sole duty financial and accounting personnel;

4. Enterprises which apply to accept or handle foreign advertisements must have the capability to handle foreign advertising.

Article 4.   Those public institutions which concurrently undertake advertising business must conform with the following conditions:

1. Having the means to publish advertisements directly and the technology of designing and production and equipment;

2. Having managing personnel who are familiar with the RAM and copy editors;

3. Having individual account books and sole-duty or part-time financial and accounting personnel.

Article 5.   Joint ventures or cooperative ventures which apply for running advertising business can refer to the related articles of RAM and these detailed rules.

Article 6.   Individual operators who apply to handle advertising business must have professional advertising techniques, be familiar with the RAM and pass an examination and censor besides conforming with the conditions stipulated in "Provisional Control Regulations of Urban and Rural Individual Operators."

Article 7.   According to the stipulations of Article 6 of RAM, the following procedures must be followed when applying for censorship and registration:

1. National advertising enterprises, joint ventures, cooperative venture advertising enterprises: apply to State Administration of Industry and Commerce. When approved, a business certificate of the People's Republic of China will be given.

   Advertising enterprises of local nature: apply to local municipal or county administrative bureau of industry and commerce and report to provincial, autonomous region, municipality directly under the Central Government Administration of Industry and Commerce, or its authorized administration of industry and commerce of municipality under provincial government for approval. When approved, an Enterprise Corporation Business Certificate will be given by the municipal or county administration of industry and commerce where the applicant is situated.

2. Those public institutions which concurrently undertake advertising business: apply to local municipal or county administrative bureau of industry and commerce and report to provincial, autonomous region, municipality directly under the Central Government Administration of Industry and Commerce, or its authorized administration of industry and commerce of municipality under provincial government for approval. When approved, a permit for running advertising business will be given by the municipal or county Administration of Industry and Commerce where the applicant is situated.

   Public institutions which concurrently undertake advertising business apply to handle directly foreign advertising: apply to provincial, autonomous region, municipality directly under the Central Government Administration of Industry and Commerce. After being censored and reported to State Administration of Industry and Commerce and approved, a business certificate of the People's Republic of China will be given by provincial, autonomous region, municipality directly under the Central Government Administration of Industry and Commerce.

3. Individual operator handling advertising business: apply to the local municipal or county administration of industry and commerce and report to the provincial, autonomous region, or municipality directly under the Central Government Administration of Industry and Commerce, or its authorized administration of industry and commerce of municipality under provincial government for approval. When approved, a business license will be given by the municipal or county administration of industry and commerce where the applicant is situated.

4. When sponsoring temporary local advertising activities, the sponsor should apply to provincial, autonomous region, municipality directly under the Central Government Administration of Industry and Commerce, or its authorized administration of industry and commerce of municipality under provincial government for approval. When approved, a permit for temporary advertising business will be given.

   When sponsoring temporary national advertising activities, the sponsor should apply to provincial, autonomous region, or municipality directly under the Central Government Administration of Industry and Commerce and report to State Administration of Industry and Commerce for approval. When approved, a permit for temporary advertising business will be given by the provincial, autonomous region, municipality directly under the Central Government Administration of Industry and Commerce where the sponsor is situated.

Article 8. Public institutions which concurrently undertake advertising business, when approved, can handle advertising business of media of the same category.

Article 9. Advertisers that apply for advertising cigarettes in media other than radio broadcasting, TV, and publications must get the approval of provincial, autonomous region, or municipality directly under the Central Government Administration of Industry and Commerce or its authorized administration of industry and commerce of municipality under provincial government.

Advertisers that apply for advertising high-quality spirit winning prize from State, Department, or provincial level organization must get the approval of provincial, autonomous region or municipality directly under the Central Government Administration of Industry and Commerce or its authorized administration of industry and commerce of municipality under provincial government.

When publishing advertisements of wines under 39 degree (including 39 degree) must specify the degree of wine.

Article 10.   According to the stipulations of Article 7 of RAM, advertisers must submit the related certificates for verification when applying for publishing of advertisements:

1. Industrial and Commercial enterprises and individual operators: duplicate of business certificate of enterprise corporation and business license separately.

2. Organizations, groups, public institutions: submit their own testimonial.

3. Individuals: submit testimonial of county or town People's Government, subdistrict office, or the organization in which the individual is employed.

4. National corporations, joint ventures, cooperative ventures, foreign sole proprietorship enterprises: submit business certificate of the People's Republic of China issued by State Administration of Industry and Commerce.

5. Permanent representative organization of foreign enterprise: submit the register certificate of permanent representative organization in China of foreign enterprise issued by State Administration of Industry and Commerce.

Article 11.   According to Article 11 (1), when applying to publish advertising of commodities, testimonials certifying conformation with State Standard, Department Standard (Speciality Standard) enterprise's standard of quality must be submitted for verification.

Article 12.   According to the stipulations of Article 11 (2) of RAM, when applying to publish advertisement of prize-winning commodities, certificate proving the prize awarding issued by administrative organ above the provincial, autonomous region, municipality directly under the Central Government level must be submitted for verification.

Article 13. According to the stipulations of Article 11 (7) of RAM related testimonial must be presented:

1. Advertisement of publishing and circulating of newspapers and publications: submit the registration form issued by news and publishing organization of provincial, autonomous region, municipality directly under the Central Government.

2. Advertisement of publishing of books: submit testimonial approving the establishment of publishing house issued by news and publishing organization.

3. Advertisement of various kinds of literature and art performances: testimonial issued by culture administration above the county level approving the putting on of the performance.

4. Advertisement recruiting students of colleges and universities: submit testimonial of approval to publish or broadcast such advertisement issued by State Educational Committee or educational administration of provincial, autonomous region, municipality directly under the Central Government. Middle professional training schools: submit testimonial of approval to publish or broadcast such advertisement issued by educational administration of prefectural (municipality). To publish or broadcast advertisement of foreign schools to recruit students: submit testimonial of approval issued by State Educational Committee.

5. Advertisement of various cultural continuation class or vocational technical training class to recruit students, advertisements to recruit workers and offer jobs: submit testimonials of approval to publish or broadcast such advertisement issued by above the county (including county) level educational administration or labor and personnel administration must be presented.

6. Advertisement of individual physicians: submit testimonial of approval to practice medicine and testimonial of the contents of advertisement being censored and approved by above the county (including county) health administration.

7. Advertisements of medicine and similar products: submit form of censorship of medicine advertisement issued by health administration of provincial, autonomous region, municipality directly under the Central Government where the advertiser is situated.

8. Advertisements of veterinary medicine: submit testimonial of approval issued by farming, animal husbandry and fishery administration of provincial, autonomous region, municipality directly under the Central Government.

9. Advertisements of pesticide: submit form of censorship and approval of pesticide advertisement issued by ministry of farming, husbandry and fishery, or provincial, autonomous region, municipality directly under the Central Government administration of farming, husbandry and fishery, or department of medicine inspection or plantation protection.

Article 14. According to the stipulations of Article 11 (8) of RAM, when applying to publish or broadcast advertisements of the following contents, related testimonials must be submitted:

1. Advertisement of food: submit form of censorship and approval of food advertisement issued by local food hygienic supervising organization above the municipal level.

2. Advertisement of various kinds of exhibitions, order-taking meetings, fairs: submit testimonial of approval of the department responsible for the work of the sponsor.

3. Advertisement of savings with prizes: submit testimonial of People's Bank of one level higher.

4. Notice or proclamation of individuals: submit testimonial of the organization in which the individual is employed or county or town people's government or subdistrict office.

Article 15. When applying to publish, broadcast, erect, or post advertisements, the advertiser must submit the originals of the testimonials or reproduction of the testimonials with the signature and chop of the organization which issued the testimonial and notarized by the notarization organization.

Article 16. According to the stipulations of Article 15 of RAM the service charge for handling domestic advertising is 10 percent of the advertising fee; the handling charge paid to foreign firms for handling foreign advertising in China is 15 percent of the advertising fee.

Article 17.   Foreign enterprises (organizations) or foreigners soliciting and publishing advertisements ought to authorize the execution to the advertising operator having the right to handle foreign advertising.

Article 18.   According to the stipulations of Article 12 of RAM, those who handle and publish the advertisement must both be responsible to censor the contents of advertisement, verify the related testimonials, and have the right to ask the advertiser to submit other necessary testimonial documents. It is not allowed to handle and publish advertisement without legal testimonials, or if the testimonials are incomplete or the contents of the advertisement are truthless.

Advertising operators must set up a system of registration of solicitation, reexamination and business record. The duration of keeping the record is not less than one year.

Article 19.   If an advertiser violates Article 3, Article 8 (5) of the RAM using advertising to practice fraud to cheat the users and consumers, the advertiser is ordered to publish make-correction advertisement within certain circle; and according to the condition a fine of more than twofold to less than fivefold of the advertising fee is to be made. When harm is done to the users and consumers, the responsibility of compensation is to be borne by the advertiser.

If the advertising operator helps its client to practice fraud, the following steps are to be taken according to the condition: circulate a notice of criticism, confiscate its income, fine more than twofold to less than fivefold of the advertising fee. When the advertising operator violates continuously and does not make corrections, his business is to be stopped and reorganized; cancel its business license to run advertising business. If harm is done to the users and consumers, joint responsibility of compensation is to be borne.

To publish make-correction advertisement, the cost is to be borne by the advertiser and advertising operator respectively.

Article 20.   Those who violate the stipulations in Article 4 and Article 8 (6) of RAM, the following steps are to be taken according to the condition: circulate a notice of criticism, confiscate the income, a fine of under 5,000 yuan or order to stop business and reorganize.

Article 21.   Advertising operator, which violates the stipulations in Article 6 of RAM, has no license or run advertising business beyond the scope of advertising business, ban its illegal business activities, confiscate its illegal income, make a fine of below 5,000 yuan.

Article 22.   When the advertiser violates the stipulations of Article 7 of RAM, a notice of criticism is to be circulated, a fine of below 5,000 yuan is to be made according to the condition.

Article 23.   When the advertising operator violates the stipulations in Article 8 (1), (2), (3), (4) of RAM, a notice of criticism to be circulated, illegal income be confiscated, a fine of below 10,000 yuan be made; in the case of the advertiser, a notice of criticism to be circulated, a fine of below twofold of the advertising fee be made according to the condition.

Article 24.   When news media violate the stipulations in Article 9 of RAM, a notice of criticism to be circulated, illegal income be confiscated, a fine of below 10,000 yuan be made according to the condition.

Article 25.   When the advertising operator violates the stipulations in Article 10 of RAM, notice of criticism to be circulated, illegal income be confiscated, a fine of below 10,000 yuan be made according to the condition.

Article 26.   Advertiser violates the stipulations in Article 11 of RAM by falsifying, altering, embezzling, or illegally reproducing advertising testimonials, a notice of criticism to be circulated, a fine of below 5,000 yuan to be made.

When advertising operator violates the stipulations in Article 11 (2), (3), a fine of below 1,000 yuan to be made.

To present illegal or false testimonials for the client, a notice of criticism to be circulated, a fine of below 5,000 yuan to be made and joint responsibility should be borne.

Article 27.   When advertising operator violates the stipulations in Article 12 of RAM, a notice of criticism to be circulated, illegal income to be confiscated, a fine of below 3,000 yuan to be made; when resulting in a false advertisement, make-correction advertisement must be published; when causing harm to the users and consumers, joint responsibility of compensation is to be borne.

Article 28.   When violating the stipulations in Article 13 of RAM by illegally erecting, posting advertisements, illegal income to be confiscated, a fine of below 5,000 yuan to be made and the advertisement should be taken down in a limited time. If not taken down in time, the advertisement is to be taken down by force, its cost to be borne by the party which erected, posted the advertisement.

Article 29.   When the stipulations in Article 14 and Article 15 of RAM are violated, a notice of criticism is to be circulated, to make correction in a limited time to be ordered, the illegal income to be confiscated, a fine of below 5,000 yuan to be made.

Article 30.   When foreign enterprise or regular representative organization of foreign enterprise violates the stipulations of RAM, provincial, autonomous region, municipality directly under the Central Government Administration of Industry and Commerce where the enterprise or organization is situated makes proposal of handling the case by referring to the articles of these detailed rules, reports to the State Administration of Industry and Commerce and takes action when approved.

Article 31.   The State Administration of Industry and Commerce is responsible to make explanations of the Detailed Rules.

Article 32.   The Detailed Rules shall come into force as from the date of promulgation.

Appendix IV

Provisions of the State Council of the People's Republic of China for the Encouragement of Foreign Investment*

Article 1. These provisions are hereby formulated in order to improve the investment environment, facilitate the absorption of foreign investment, introduce advanced technology, improve product quality, expand exports in order to generate foreign exchange, and develop the national economy.

Article 2. The State encourages foreign companies, enterprises, and other economic entities or individuals (hereinafter referred to as "foreign investors") to establish Chinese-foreign equity joint ventures, Chinese-foreign cooperative ventures and wholly foreign-owned enterprises (hereinafter referred to as "enterprises with foreign investment") within the territory of China.

*Promulgated on October 11, 1986.

The State grants special preferences to the enterprises with foreign investment listed below:

1. Production enterprises whose products are mainly for export, which have a foreign exchange surplus after deducting from their total annual foreign exchange revenues the annual foreign exchange expenditures incurred in production and operation and the foreign exchange needed for the remittance abroad of the profits earned by foreign investors (hereinafter referred to as "export enterprises").

2. Production enterprises possessing advanced technology supplied by foreign investors which are engaged in developing new products, and upgrading and replacing products in order to increase foreign exchange generated by exports or for import substitution (hereinafter referred to as "technologically advanced enterprises").

Article 3. Export enterprises and technology advanced enterprises shall be exempt from payment to the state of all subsidies to staff and workers, except for the payment of or allocation of funds for labor insurance, welfare costs, and housing subsidies for Chinese staff and workers in accordance with the provisions of the state.

Article 4. The site use fees for export enterprises and technologically advanced enterprises, except for those located in busy urban sectors of large cities, shall be computed and charged according to the following standards:

1. Five to twenty RMB yuan per square meter per year in areas where the development fee and the site use fee are computed and charged together;

2. Not more than three RMB yuan per square meter per year in site areas where the development fee is computed and charged on a one-time basis or areas which are developed by the above-mentioned enterprises themselves.

Exemptions for specified periods of time from the fees provided in the foregoing provision may be granted at the discretion of local people's governments.

Article 5. Export enterprises and technologically advanced enterprises shall be given priority in obtaining water, electricity, and transportation services, and communication facilities needed for their production and operation. Fees shall be computed and charged in accordance with the standards for local state enterprises.

Article 6.   Export enterprises and technologically advanced enterprises, after examination by the Bank of China, shall be given priority in receiving loans for short-term revolving funds needed for production and distribution, as well as for other needed credit.

Article 7.   When foreign investors in export enterprises and technologically advanced enterprises remit abroad profits distributed to them by such enterprises, the amount remitted shall be exempt from income tax.

Article 8.   After the expiration of the period for the reduction or exemption of enterprise income tax in accordance with the provisions of the State, export enterprises whose value of export products in that year amounts to 70 percent or more of the value of their products for that year, may pay enterprise income tax at one-half the rate of the present tax.

Export enterprises in the special economic zones and in the economic and technological development zones and other export enterprises that already pay enterprise income tax at a tax rate of 15 percent and that comply with the foregoing conditions, shall pay enterprise income tax at a rate of 10 percent.

Article 9.   After the expiration of the period of reduction or exemption of enterprise income tax in accordance with the provisions of the State, technologically advanced enterprises may extend for three years the payment of enterprise income tax at a rate reduced by one half.

Article 10.   Foreign investors who reinvest the profits distributed to them by their enterprises in order to establish or expand export enterprises or technologically advanced enterprises for a period of operation of not less than five years, after application to and approval by the tax authorities, shall be refunded the total amount of enterprise income tax already paid on the reinvested portion. If the investment is withdrawn before the period of operation reaches five years, the amount of enterprise income tax refunded shall be repaid.

Article 11. Export products of enterprises with foreign investment, except crude oil, finished oil, and other products subject to special State provisions, shall be exempt from the consolidated industrial and commercial tax.

Article 12. Enterprises with foreign investment may arrange the export of their products directly or may also export by consignment to agents in accordance with State provisions. For products that require an export license, in accordance with the annual export plan of the enterprise, an application for an export license may be made every six months.

Article 13. Machinery and equipment, vehicles used in production, raw materials, fuel, bulk parts, spare parts, machine component parts, and fittings (including imports restricted by the State), which enterprises with foreign investment need to import in order to carry out their export contracts do not require further applications for examination and approval and are exempt from the requirement for import licenses. The customs department shall exercise supervision and control, and shall inspect and release such imports on the basis of the enterprise contract or the export contract.

The imported materials and items mentioned above are restricted to use by the enterprise and may not be sold on the domestic market. If they are used in products to be sold domestically, import procedures shall be handled in accordance with provisions and the taxes shall be made up according to the governing sections.

Article 14. Under the supervision of the foreign exchange control departments, enterprises with foreign investment may mutually adjust their foreign exchange surpluses and deficiencies among each other.

The Bank of China and other banks designated by the People's Bank of China may provide cash security services and may grant loans in Renminbi to enterprises with foreign investment.

Article 15. The people's governments at all levels and relevant departments in charge shall guarantee the right of autonomy of enterprises with foreign investment and shall support enterprises with foreign investment in managing themselves in accordance with international advanced scientific methods.

With the scope of their approved contracts, enterprises with foreign investment have the right to determine by themselves production and operation plans, to raise funds, to use funds, to purchase production materials, and to sell products; and to determine by themselves the wage levels, the forms of wages, and bonuses and the allowance system.

Enterprises with foreign investment may, in accordance with their production and operation requirements, determine by themselves their organizational structure and personnel system, employ or dismiss senior management personnel, increase or dismiss staff and workers. They may recruit and employ technical personnel, managerial personnel, and workers in their locality. The unit to which such employed personnel belong shall provide its support and shall permit their transfer. Staff and workers who violate the rules and regulations, and thereby cause certain bad consequences may, in accordance with the seriousness of the case, be given differing sanctions, up to that of discharge. Enterprises with foreign investment that recruit, employ, dismiss, or discharge staff and workers, shall file a report with the local labor and personnel department.

Article 16.   All districts and departments must implement the "Circular of the State Council concerning Firmly Curbing the Indiscriminate Levy of Charges on Enterprises." The people's governments at the provincial level shall formulate specific methods and strengthen supervision and administration.

Enterprises with foreign investment that encounter unreasonable charges may refuse to pay and may also appeal to the local economic committees up to the State Economic Commission.

Article 17.   The people's governments at all levels and relevant departments in charge shall strengthen the coordination of their work, improve efficiency in handling matters and shall promptly examine and approve matters reported by enterprises with foreign investment that require response and resolution. The agreement, contract, and articles of association of an enterprise with foreign investment shall be examined and approved by the departments in charge under the State Council. The examination and approval authority must within three months from the date of receipt of all documents decide to approve or not to approve them.

Article 18.   Export enterprises and technologically advanced enterprises mentioned in these provisions shall be confirmed jointly as such by the foreign economic relations and trade departments where such enterprises are located and the relevant departments in accordance with the enterprise contract, and certification shall be issued.

If the actual results of the annual exports of an export enterprise are unable to realize the goal of the surplus in the foreign exchange balance that is stipulated in the enterprise contract, the taxes and fees which have already been reduced or exempted in the previous year shall be made up in the following year.

Article 19. Except where these provisions expressly provide that they are to be applicable to export enterprises or technologically advanced enterprises, other articles shall be applicable to all enterprises with foreign investment.

These provisions apply from the date of implementation to those enterprises with foreign investment that have obtained approval for establishment before the date of implementation of these provisions and that qualify for the preferential terms of these provisions.

Article 20. For enterprises invested in and established by companies, enterprises and other economic organizations or individuals from Hong Kong, Macao, or Taiwan, matters shall be handled by reference to these provisions.

Article 21. The Ministry of Foreign Economic Relations and Trade shall be responsible for interpreting these provisions.

Article 22. These provisions shall go into effect on the date of issue.

Appendix V

Import and Export Corporations and Enterprises of Various Ministries under the State Council

Beijing Ever Bright Industrial Company, Changguanlou, No. 143, Xizhimenwai Street, Beijing. Trust business accepting trust from various departments of the government and from provinces, autonomous regions, municipalities, and enterprises for the import of advanced technology, equipment, etc. Telex: 20023 BERIC CN.

Carrie Enterprises Ltd., 12 Xinjian Lane, West Town District, Beijing. Import and export of electronics, machinery, etc. Telex: 22068 CRI CN.

China Abrasives Export Corporation, Zhong Yuan Xi Street, Zhengzhou, Henan Province. Telex: 22546 CAECZ CN.

China Business Marine Corporation, Ltd., Import Building, Er Li Gou, Xijiao, Beijing. Telex: 22866 TRANS CN.

China Carpet Import and Export Corporation, 82, Tung An Men Street, Beijing. Telex: 22896 TUHSU CN.

China Communications Import and Export Service Company, 10, Fuxing Road, Beijing. Telex: 22462 COMOT CN.

China Diamonds and Jewelry Import and Export Corporation, 82, Tung An Men Street, Beijing. Telex: 22155 CHART CN.

China Economic and Trade Consultants Corporation, 7, Guanghua Road, Jian Guo Men Wai, Beijing. Telex: 22506 CTSUL CN.

China Economic Development Corporation, 93, Bei He Yan Dajie, Beijing. Organizes joint venture, coproduction, processing, assembling, and compensation trade for domestic and foreign firms or units. Telex: 22044 ACFIC CN.

China Educational Instrument and Equipment Corporation, 35, Damucang Lane, West District, Beijing.

China Electro-Ceramic Export Allied Corporation, Yanziji, Nanjing. Telex: 34121 ZDCNJ CN.

China Engineering Technology Development Corporation, 7, Tou Tiao, Nan Li Shi Road, Fu Xing Men Wai Street, Beijing. Telex: 22095 CIECC CN.

China Film Equipment Corporation, 25, Xin Jie Kou Wai Street, Beijing. Cable: 33745 BEIJING.

China Film Export and Import Corporation, 25, Xin Jie Kou Wai Street, Beijing. Telex: 22195 FILM CN.

China Flowers Import and Export Corporation, Lu Son Yuan Hotel, 22 Banchang Hutung, Jiaodao Kou, Beijing. Cable: 4278 BEIJING.

China Foreign Economic Relations and Trade Publishing House, 28, Dong Hou Xiang, An Ding Men Wai Street, Beijing. Telex: 22168 MFTPK CN.

China Fu Li Company, 1 (A), Da Hua Road, Dong Dan, Beijing. Handles the import of electronic product, machinery and equipment, etc. Telex: 22427 BHCTL CN.

China Gold Dragon Company, Room No. 3208 Yanjing Hotel, Beijing. Imports electronics, machinery, equipment and instruments. Telex: 22767 CGDC CN.

China Great Wall Industry Corporation, 17 Wen Chang Hutong, Beijing. Accepts orders for the development, production, and launching of application satellites, and rocket carriers, etc. Telex: 22651 CGWIC CN.

China Guangan Engineering Consulting Corporation, 4, Baiguang Road, Beijing. Telex: 22602 CEC CN.

China Harbors Engineering Company, Fuxing Road, Beijing. Telex: 20029 CHEC CN.

China Hua Jian Company, 5, Shun Yuan Jie, San Yuan Qiao, Dong Zhi Men Wai, Beijing. Brings in capital and investment, advanced technology, and equipment of economic organizations and individuals from Hong Kong, Macao, Taiwan, and foreign countries. Telex: 22539 CGHC CH.

China Hua Yang Technology and Trade Corporation, 4/F, Cultural Palace of Nationalities, Beijing. Telex: 22536 NBO CN.

China Import and Export Corporation of State Farms, 56, Zhuanta Hutong, Xisi, Beijing. Telex: 20034 CALF CN.

Ching Interior Design and Decoration Material Import and Export Corporation, A-2, Hou Niu Rou Wan, Xi Dan, Beijing. Telex: 210207 SURDD CN.

China International Advertising Corporation, 19, Shao Jiu Hutong, Wangfujing Street, Beijing. Telex: 222622 CIACO CN.

China International Book Trading Corporation, 21, Che Gong Zhuang, West Road, Beijing. Telex: 22496 CIBTC CN.

China International Cooperation Company for Agriculture, Livestock, and Fishery, 56, Zhuanta Hutong, Xisi, Beijing. Telex: 20034 CALF CN.

China International Economic and Technical Cooperative Consultants, 1, Fu Xing Men Wai Street, Beijing. Telex: 22315 CCPIT CN.

China International Economic Consultants, 2/F CITIC Building, 19 Jianguomenwai Dajie, Beijing. Telex: 22994 CIEC CN.

China International Exhibition Center, Jing An Zhuang, North 3rd, Rin Road, Chao Yang District, Beijing. Telex: 22315 CCPIT CN.

China International Packaging Technology Trading Corporation, 4, Guan Yi Street, Xuanwu District, Beijing. Telex: 22234 CNPC CN.

China International Television Cooperation Corporation, 15 Hu Fang Lu, Beijing. Cable: 3502 BEIJING.

China International Television Corporation, 2, Fuxinmenwai Street, Beijing. Telex: 22235 CCTV CN.

China International Water and Electric Corporation, Liu Pu Kang, Beijing. Telex: 22485 WATER CN.

China Jing An Equipment Import and Export Corporation, 43, Xi Tang Zi Lane, North Wang Fu Jing Street, Beijing. Telex: 210020 CJIMC CN.

China Jing Xi Engineering Consulting Corporation, 12, Fu Xing Avenue, Beijing. Telex: 22194 GDINM CN.

China Kang Hua Investment and Import and Export Corporation, 20, Nei Wu Bu Street, Beijing. Exports leather and products of leather, etc., and imports electronic equipment, etc. Telex: 210065 KHIN CN.

China Light Industrial Corporation for Foreign Economic and Technical Cooperation, 22B, Fu Wai Da Jie, Beijing. Telex: 22465 LIMEX CN.

China Metallurgical Import and Export Corporation, 46 Dongsixi Dajia, Beijing. Telex: 22461 MIEC CN.

China National Aero-Technology Import and Export Corporation, 67, Jiao Nan Street, Beijing. Telex: 22318 AEROT CN.

China National Agricultural Machinery Import and Export Corporation, 26, South Yuetan Street, Beijing. Telex: 22467 AMPRC CN.

China National Animal Breeding Stock Import and Export Corporation, Hepingli, Beijing. Telex: 22233 MAAF CN Attention CABS.

China National Arts and Crafts Import and Export Corporation, 82, Tung An Men Street, Beijing. Telex: 22155 CNART CN.

China National Automotive Industry Import and Export Corporation, 27, Liu Yin Street, West District, Beijing. Telex: 22092 CAIEC CN.

China National Bearing Joint Export Corporation, 12, Fu Xing Men Wai Street, Beijing. Telex: 22534 BREXP CN.

China National Cereals, Oils, and Foodstuffs Import and Export Corporation, 82, Dong An Men Street, Beijing. Telex: 22281 CEROF CN, 22111 CEROF CN.

China National Chartering Corporation, Import Building, Er Li Gou, Xijiao, Beijing. Telex: 22265 CHART CN.

China National Chemical Construction Corporation, Building 16, Qi Qu, Hepingli, Beijing. Telex: 22492 CNCCC CN.

China National Chemicals Import and Export Corporation, Erligou, Xijiao, Beijing. Telex: 22243 CHEMI CN.

China National Complete Plant Export Corporation, 28, Donghouxiang, Andingmen Wai, Beijing. Telex: 22559 COMPT CN.

China National Consumer Electrics and Electronics Corporation, 82, Tung An Men Street, Beijing. Telex: 210031 LIGHT CN.

China National Corporation of Pharmaceutical Economic and Technical International Cooperation, Jinsong Shabanzhuang, Beijing. Telex: 22659 SPAC CN.

China National Electric Wire and Cable Export Corporation, Langjia Yuan, Jianguomenwai, Beijing. Telex: 22614 CCC CN.

China National Electronics Import and Export Corporation, 49, Fuxing Road, Beijing. Telex: 22475 CEIEC CN.

China National Embroidery and Drawn Work Associated Export Corporation, 82, Tung An Men Street, Beijing. Telex: 22155 CNART CN.

China National Foreign Trade Transportation Corporation, Import Building, Er Li Gou, Xijiao, Beijing. Telex: 22863 TRANS CN.

China National Import and Export Commodities Inspection Corporation, 12, Jian Guo Men Wai Street, Beijing. Telex: 210076 SACI CN.

China National Instruments Import and Export Corporation, Erligou, Xijiao, Beijing. Telex: 22304 CIIEC CN.

China National Light Industrial Products Import and Export Corporation, 82, Tung An Men Street, Beijing. Telex: 22282 LIGHT CN.

China National Light Industrial Products Import Technical Service Center, 2 Yabao Lu, Chaoyang District, Beijing. Cable: 6083 BEIJING.

China National Machinery and Equipment Import and Export Corporation, 12, Fu Xing Men Wai Street, Beijing. Telex: 22186 EQUIP CN.

China National Machinery Import and Export Corporation, Erligou, Xijiao, Beijing. Telex: 22242 CMIEC CN.

China National Material Supply Corporation, Shou, Du Ti Yu Guan, Hai Dian District, Beijing. Telex: 22241 MIMET CN.

China National Medical Equipment and Supply Import and Export Corporation, 44 Houhai Beiyan, Beijing. Telex: 22193 MINIH CN.

China National Medicines and Health Products Import and Export Corporation, Building No. 12, Jiangoumenwai Street, Beijing. Telex: 20046 MEHEC CN.

China National Metals and Minerals Import and Export Corporation, Erligou, Xijiao, Beijing. Telex: 22241 MIMET CN.

China National Metals Products Import and Export Corporation, Erligou, Xijiao, Beijing. Telex: 22241 MIMET CN.

China National Native Produce and Animal By-products Import and Export Corporation, 82, Tung An Men Street, Beijing. Telex: 22283 TUHSU CN.

China National New Building Materials Import and Export Corporation, Zi Zhu Yuan Road, Xi Jiao, Beijing. Telex: 20038 CNBMC CN.

China National Nonferrous Metals Import and Export Corporation, 9, Xizhang Hutong, Xizhimennei Street, Beijing. Telex: 22086 CNIEC CN.

China National Offshore Oil Corporation, 31, Dong Chang An Jie, Beijing. Telex: 22611 CNOOC CN.

China National Overseas Chinese Tourism Commodity and Remittance Service Corporation, A-3 Jian Guo Men Wai Street, Beijing. Telex: 22487 CTSHO CN.

China National Packaging Import and Export Corporation, 28, Dong Hou Xiang, An Ding Men Wai, Beijing. Telex: 22490 CPACK CN.

China National Philatelic Corporation, 2, Xuan Wumen East Street, Beijing. Telex: 22026 STAMP CN.

China National Postal and Telecommunications Appliances Corporation, 13, West Chang An Avenue, Beijing. Telex: Import Department, CPTAC CN.

China National Publications Import and Export Corporation, 137 Chao Nei Dajie, Beijing. Telex: 22313 CPC CN.

China National Publishing Industry Trading Corporation, P.O. Box 782, No. 504, An Jua Li, An Ding Men Wai, Beijing. Telex: 22497 NPAPC CN.

China National Pulp and Paper Corporation, 82, Tung An Men Street, Beijing. Telex: 22048 LIGHT CN.

China National Seed Corporation, 16, Dong Huan Bei Road, Beijing. Telex: 22233 MAAF CN CNSC.

China National Silk Import and Export Corporation, 82, Tung An Men Street, Beijing. Telex: 22652 CSCBJ CN.

China National Technical Import Corporation, Erligou, Xijiao, Beijing. Telex: 22244 CNTIC CN.

China National Textiles Import and Export Corporation, 82, Tung An Men Street, Beijing. Telex: 22280 CNTEX CN.

China North Industries Corporation, 7A, Yuetan Street S, Beijing. Exports, various kinds of heavy machinery, special equipment, etc. Telex: 22339 CNIC CN.

China Nuclear Energy Industry Corporation, P.O. Box 2139, 21 Nanlishilu, Beijing. Telex: 22240 CNEIC CN.

China Ocean Helicopter Corporation, Nantou Heliport, Shenzhen City, Guangdong Province. Telex: (COHC) 44250 COHCH CN.

China Ocean Shipping Agency Head Office, 6, Dong Chang An Street, Beijing. Telex: 22264 CPCPK CN.

China Ocean Shipping Company Head Office, 6, Dong Chang An Street, Beijing. Telex: 22264 CPCPK CN.

China Overseas Trading Company, Ltd., 11, Jianhua Nan Lu, Jianguo Men Wai, Beijing. Telex: 210202 COTCO CN.

China Petro-Chemical International Company, Building 2, 5 Qu, Hepingli, Beijing. Telex: 22655 CPCCI CN.

China Petroleum Engineering Construction Corporation, Liu Pu Kang, Beijing. Telex: 20047 CPECC CN.

China Rainbow Development Corporation, Building B 12, District 7, He Ping Li, Beijing. Invests both in exploration and development of the mineral resources at home and abroad. Telex: 210038 CRDC CN.

China Record Corporation, 2, Fuxing Men Wai Street, Beijing. Telex: 22236 RTPRC CN.

China Rural and Town Enterprises Import and Export Company, 16, Dong Huan Bei Lu, Beijing. Cable: 8046 BEIJING.

China Service Center for Friendship and Cooperation with Foreign Countries, 1, Tai Ji Chang, Beijing. Cable CSCFCO.

China Service Corporation for Chinese Personnel Working Abroad, 28, Dong Hou Xiang, Andingmen Wai, Beijing. Telex: 22559 COMPT CN.

China Shipbuilding Trading Company, Ltd., 10 Yuetan Beixiaojie, Beijing. Telex: 22335 CSSC CN.

China Silk Materials Import Corporation, 82, Tung An Men Street, Beijing. Telex: 210081 CSMIC CN.

China Southwest Energy United Development Corporation, 16, He Ping North Street, Hepingli, Beijing. Telex: 210044 CSUDC CN.

China State Construction Engineering Corporation, Bai Wan Zhuang, Beijing. Telex: 22477 CSCEC CN.

China Tea Import and Export Corporation, 82, Tung An Men Street, Beijing. Telex: 22899 TUHSU CN.

China Tex Accessories Import and Export Corporation, 201, Wang Fu Jing Street, Beijing. Telex: 210026 CNACS CN.

China Tex Raw Materials Import and Export Corporation, 20, Wang Fu Jing Street, Beijing. Telex: 210025 CNTEX CN.

China Textile Industrial Corporation for Foreign Economic and Technical Cooperation, 12, East Chang An Street, Beijing. Telex: 22661 MTI CN.

China Textile Machinery and Technology Import and Export Corporation, 12, East Chang An Street, Beijing. Telex: 22661 MTI CN.

China Timber Import and Export Corporation, A-2, Hou Niu Rou Wan, Xi Dan, Beijing. Telex: 22898 TIMEX CN.

China Tobacco Import and Export Corporation, 67, You An Men Street, Beijing. Telex: 22015 CNTC CN.

China United Animals and Poultry Corporation, 82, Tung An Men Street, Beijing. Telex: 22281 CEROF CN.

China United Electric Export Corporation, 60, Le Pei Yuan, Guang An Men Nei Street, Beijing. Telex: 22620 CUEC CN.

China Wan Bao Engineering Corporation, 7, Yuetan Nanjie, Beijing. Contracts for construction and technical upgrading of plants, etc. Telex: 22985 CNWB CN.

China Xiao Feng Technology and Equipment Company, 92, Dongzhimennei Dajie, Beijing. Telex: 22499 CIFIC CN.

China Xinshidai Company, P.O. Box 1092, Beijing. Imports and exports nuclear industry products, aircraft products, electronics, ships, etc. Telex: 22338 XSDCO CN.

China Xinxing Corporation, Shou Song Hotel, Wan Shou Road, Beijing. Telex: 22062 CXXC CN.

China Yangtze Grinding Machine Export, Inc., 1146, Jungong Road, Shanghai. Telex: 33097 SMTW CN.

China Zhen Hua Import and Export Corporation, Room 1514, Beijing Hotel, Beijing. Handles electronics, communication, space technology, aviation, navigation equipment, etc.

China Zhen Xing Economy and Trading Corporation, 73, Bensi Lane, Dong Si Nan Dai Jie, Beijing. Telex: 210015 BZETCC CN.

China Zhihua Corporation, Ltd., A-20, Fuxing Road, Beijing. A state-owned trading corporation to carry out technical exchanges and commercial negotiations. Telex: 22098 CZHLC CN.

Foreign Economic and Trade Consultants Corporation of All China Federation of Supply and Marketing Cooperatives, 45, Fu Xing Men Nei Street, Beijing. Telex: 222212 CFSMC CN.

International Tendering Company of China National Technical Import Corporation, Building No. 9, Xiyuan Hotel, Erligou, Beijing. Telex: 22075 CNTIC CN.

Oriental Scientific Instruments Import and Export Corporation, 52 San-li-he Road, Beijing. Telex: 20063 OSIC CN.

People's Insurance Company of China, 22 Xi Jiao Min Xiang, Beijing. Telex: 22102 PICC CN.

Ping He Electronics Company, Ltd., 19 (A) Gong Men Kou Er Tiao, Fu Cheng Men Nei Street, Beijing. Telex: 20040 PHCL CN.

Poly Technologies Incorporated, Friendship Halls No. 1 and 2, Beijing Hotel, Beijing. Telex: 22010 POLY CN.

Qing An International Trade Company, Ltd., 1, Si Dao Kou, Xi Wai, Hai Dian District, Beijing. Imports and exports technology for energy resources, chemical and petrochemical products, machinery and equipment, electronic and communication products, etc. Telex: 20443 BNSBJ CN.

Shen Zhou Economic and Technical Development Corporation, 6 Fu Zhou Kwan Chienjie, Beijing. Engaged in application of foreign funds, importing technology, acquisition of foreign mental and information resources, developing technoeconomy at home and abroad, and providing consultant services. Telex: 210063 EDTON c/o Shen-Zhou.

Spares and Components Company of China National Technical Import Corporation, Hou Niu Rou Wan Az, Xi Dan, Beijing. Telex: 22244 CNTIC CN.

Surveying and Mapping Technology Corporation of China, Baiwanz-huang, Beijing. Telex: 22477 CSCEC CN.

Technical Service Company of China National Instruments Import and Export Corporation, Beijing Exhibition Center. Telex: 22304 CIIEC CN.

Technology Trading Consultant Company of China National Technical Import Corporation, Che Gong Zhuang Bei Li No. 55, Zhanlan Road, Beijing. Telex: 22244 CNTIC CN.

Bibliography and Sources

Books, Republic of China Publishers

Bai Shouyi, ed. *An Outline History of China*. Beijing, China: Foreign Language Press, 1982.

China ABC. Beijing, China: New World Press.

China: A General Survey. Beijing, China: Foreign Language Press, 1982.

China: An Introduction. Beijing, China: Foreign Language Press, 1984.

China Features. Beijing, China: China Feature Institute, 1987.

China News Yearbook 1983. Beijing, China: China Social Science Academy Publishing House, 1983.

China News Yearbook 1984. Beijing, China: Publishing House of People's Daily, 1984.

China's Progress in Advertising. Shanghai, China: China Commercial Advertising Agency, 1936.

China Today No. 3. Beijing, China: Beijing Review Publications, 1982.

Culture. Beijing, China: Foreign Language Press, 1982.

Dun J. Li, translator. *History.* Beijing, China: Foreign Language Press (Editorial Committee of China Handbook Series), 1982.

Economic Readjustment and Reform. Beijing, China: Beijing Review Special Section Series, 1982.

Ge Gong Zhen. *History of Chinese Journalism.* Shanghai, China: Commercial Press, 1927.

Latsch, Marie Luise. *Chinese Traditional Festivals.* Beijing, China: New World Press, 1984.

Manying Ip. *The Life and Times of Zhang Yuanji.* Beijing, China: Commercial Press, 1985.

Questions and Answers about China's National Minorities. Beijing, China: New World Press.

Shanghai—Key to Modern China. Shanghai, China: Shanghai People's Publishing House, 1986.

Journals, Republic of China

China Daily. Beijing, China.

China Industry & Commerce Gazette. Beijing, China.

Economic Daily. Beijing, China.

Sin Wen Pao. Shanghai, China.

Wen Hui Bao. Shanghai, China.

World Economic Herald. Shanghai, China.

Xin Min Evening News. Shanghai, China.

Books, U.S. Publishers

Buell, Victor P. *Marketing Management.* McGraw-Hill, 1984.

Journals, U.S. Publishers

Advertising Age. June 9, 1986, October 27, 1986.

Media. December 16, 1988.

Miscellaneous

Directory of Chinese Foreign Economic Relations and Trade Enterprises. Beijing, China: China Foreign Economic Relations and Trade Publishing House, 1987.

Main Figures of 1982 Census. Beijing, China: China Statistical Publishing House, 1982.

1987 Annual Report. New York: International Advertising Association, 1988.

Shanghai Statistical Yearbook 1988. Shanghai, China: China Statistical Publishing House, 1988.

Souvenir Copy of Third World Advertising Congress.

Xu Bai Yi. "A Brief History of Advertising in China." 1986.

Index

Adamson, W. R. & Co., xviii
Ad mailings, xxiii
Adsale Hong Kong, 67
Advertisers, leading foreign, 65
Advertising, xvi, 33
 of American commodities, 35
 in China, xxi, 63–70
 of Chinese commodities,
  35–36
 dos and don'ts in, 90
 government regulation of, 90
 guidelines for, 85–91
 informative, 89–90
 as investment, 34
 of Japanese commodities,
  34–35
 versus personal selling, 33–34
 role of, in increasing brand-
  awareness and market share,
  43
 series, 89
 volume, 64–65
Advertising agencies, 64
 in China, xxiii

 as joint venture, 68–69
Advertising agents, foreign, 68–
  69
Advertising associations, 69
Advertising companies, major,
  66–70
Advertising industry, growth of,
  63
Advertising management,
  regulations for, 103–7,
  109–18
Advertising media, in China,
  71–83
Advertising rates
 for *China Daily*, 72
 for *People's Daily*, 72
Aeroflot Airlines, 88
Agriculture, 1, 3
Allied-Signal China, 40
All Nippon Airways, 88
American commodities,
  advertising of, 35
American Express, 68
American Motors Corporation, 9

American Snack, 32
Angel Children's Clothing Store, 26
Antaibao, 12

Banca Nazionale del Lavoro, 88
Bang Yi Peng, 58
Bank of America, 88
Bao Yu Jun, 71
Bayer China, 55, 68
Beijing, 11, 38, 40, 41, 64, 68, 83
  media reach surveys in, 79–82
Beijing Advertising Corporation, 32, 65
Beijing Automotive Works, 9
Beijing Jeep Corporation, 9
Beijing Matsushita Color Cathode Ray Tube Co., 13–14
Beijing People's Radio, 65
Beijing Philips Audio/Video Corporation, 15
Beijing Stone Electronic Company, 68
Beijing TV, 65
Bei Qing Yan Pao, xxiii
Billboards, xxii, 77
Blue Sky of Tianjin, 44
Boeing, 68, 75, 76, 83
Bovril, 56
Brand awareness, 87–88
  impact of, xvi
  role of advertising in, 43
Brand loyalty, xvi
British Airways, 88
British-American Tobacco Company, xxii, 68
Brown, Barton, 15
Buell, Victor P., 33
Bureaucrat-capitalist industries, xxv

CAAC, 68
Calcium Panthothenate Tablet, 10

Camay soap, 83, 88
Capital goods, 2
Cariplo, 88
Carl Crow, Inc., xxiii
Cathay Pacific Airlines, 88
Central People's Broadcasting Station, 74
Central People's Radio, 65
Central TV Station, 65
  advertising revenue of, 83
Central TV Surveys, 83
Changsha Refrigerator Factory, 33
Chen Zutao, 10
Chiang Kai-shek, xxiv
China
  advertising in, illustrated, 45–61
  demographic trends and buying behavior in, 24–27
  economic readjustment and reform in, 1–16
  festivals in, 24
  gross national product of, 8–9
  import and export corporations, list of, 37–38
  language in, 22–23
  population of, 17–21, 25
  solar calendar in, 23–24
China Advertising, 67
China Advertising Association, 69
China Automobile Industry Corporation, 10
China Commercial Advertising Agency (CCAA), xxiii
China Construction Machinery Corporation, 11
China Council for the Promotion of International Trade, 38–39, 69, 78
China Daily, 72–73
  advertising rate of, 72
  special supplements, 73
China Federation of Industry and Commerce, 39

China Health Care Medicine Group, 36
China Industrial and Commercial Economic Consulting Corporation (CICECC), 39
China Industry and Commerce Gazette, 34
China Institute of Social Surveys, 27
China International Advertising Corporation (CIAC), 32, 35, 66–67, 78
China International Exhibition Center (CIEC), 38, 69–70
China market, entering, 37–45
China National Advertising Association for Foreign Economic Relations and Trade, 69
China National Automotive Industry Corporation, 10, 15
China National Medicinal Corporation, 13
China Otsuka Pharmaceutical Co., Ltd., 12
China Publicity Company, xxii
China Research Center for the Promotion of Scientific and Technological Development, 27
China-Schindler Elevator Company, Ltd., 11
China–Schindler Elevator Company, Ltd., 11
China's Film Import/Export Corporation, 40
China Social Survey System (CSSS), 4
China United Lamp Company, 50
Chinese-American Cigarette Co., Ltd., 16
Chinese categories of daily life, xx
Chinese changes in lifestyle, xx

Chinese commodities, advertising of, 35–36
Chinese consumers
  buying power of, xvi
  new, xv–xvii
Chinese Lunar New Year, 24
Chinese Youth, 71
Christian Sarrazin, 12
Chrysler Motors Corporation, 12
Cigarette advertisements, 90
Cigarette production, 16
Cilek, Josef, 13
Citizen watch, 41, 90
Civil Aviation Administration of China, 14
Claude Neon Lights, xxii
Coca-Cola, 33, 40, 41, 42, 43, 44–45, 68, 75, 83
Colgate-Palmolive, 68
Commercial Press, xxii
Commodities, introduction of, to China market, 39, 40
Competition research
  in soft drink market, 41–43
  in toothpaste market, 43–44
Consolidated National Advertising Company, xxiii
Consumer goods, 2
Contac, 13
Cosmetics
  advertisements for, 90
  sales of imported, 27
Culture and Life, 74

Daiko, 68
Dai Water-Splashing Festival, 24
David Sassoon, Sons & Co., xviii
Dazhai, 29
Denmark China Food System, 38
Dentsu, 34
Deutsche Bank, 88
Di Bao (Court Gazette), xxi
Direct mail, 78
Dong Fireworks Festival, 24
Dong Yiru, 10

Double Maid, 26
Dubai, 12
Du Pont, 75, 76, 83
DYR Advertising Company, Ltd.,
    68

East China Native Products
    Exposition, xxv
Eastern Miscellany, xxii
Eastman Kodak, xxiii
Economic cooperation, future
    of, 1
Economic Daily, 71
Electronic Data Systems of
    General Motors, 39
Essix Asia Ltd., 15
Eversharp, 52
Exhibitions, 78
    effectiveness of, in introducing
        commodities, 39

Family Doctor, xxiii
Farmers, most requested goods/
    services by, 27–28
Farm machinery industry, 29
Festivals, 24
First Automobile Works of
    Changchun, 12
Five-Year Plan
    Seventh, 3, 10, 43
    Sixth, 3
Fogg, Hiram, & Co., xviii
Foreign advertisers, leading, 66
Foreign investment, magnitude
    of, in China, 11–16
Foreign label, impact of, 86–87
French Remy Martin, 40
Fujian, 83
Fuzhou Pepsi-Cola Soft Drink
    Factory, 42

General Foods, 68
General Motors, 15

Gibb, Livingston & Co., xviii
Gillette, 33, 68
Global marketing, 85
Global Vision with Local Touch, 85
Government regulation, of
    advertising, 90
Grace, W. R., and Company, 5
Grey Advertising, Inc., 68, 85
Gross national product, 8–9
Guangdong, 83
Guangdong Advertising
    Corporation, 32
Guangdong Radio, 65
Guangdong TV, 65
Guangming Daily, 71
Guangxi Province, 35
Guangzhou, 5, 41, 64, 68
Guangzhou Pepsi-Cola Soft
    Drink Factory, 42
Guangzhou Peugeot, 10
Guangzhou Tooth Paste Factory,
    44
Guangzhou Tube Factory, 44

Hainan Island, industrial and
    agricultural output, 7
Happy Home, xxii, 51
Harbin No. 3 Sweet Factory, 16
Hazeline Snow face cream, 26
Hazelwood Ice Cream, xxii
Hebei Province, 34
Heinz, 68
Henan Province, media reach
    survey in, 83
Henningsen Produce Company,
    xxii, 56, 57
Hill and Knowlton Asia Ltd., 39,
    40
Hiroji Kubota, 40
Hitachi, 83
Holiday Inn, 68
Holland Philips Transnational
    Corporation, 15
Hong Kong, 40
Hong Kong-based Adsale
    Exhibition Services, 39

Hongniang, 39
Hongqiao New Area, 5
Hua Cheng Tobacco Company, 31
Hua Ming Tobacco Company, 31
Hua Nan Sewing Machine Industrial Co., 16
Huangzi, 45
Hughes, Lyric, xv
Hyatt International, 68

Import and export corporations, lists of, 37–38, 125–33
Imports, identification of goods as, xx
Informative advertising, 89–90
International Advertisement, 67
International Advertising Association, 69
International Advertising Production Technology and Equipment Exhibition, 66–67
International Business Machines, 68
International Electric Products Exhibition, 67
International Exhibition Center, 78
International Office Equipment Exhibition, 66
International Wool Secretariat, 40, 68
Interpublic-Jardine (China) Ltd., 32, 68
Isuzu of Japan, 89
Ivory Soap, 86

JAL, 68
Janssen Pharmaceuticals Ltd., 12
Japanese commodities, advertising of, 34–35
Japanese Dentsu, 68
Japanese Hakuhodo, 68

Jardine, Matheson & Co., xviii
Jardine Schindler (Far East) Holdings SA of Hong Kong, 11
Jeep Cherokee, 9
Jiangsu, 83
Jianlibao, 43
Jie Yin, 44
Jing Bao (Peking Gazette), xxi
Jin Jiang Amusement Park, 60
Jinmen Islands, 17
Johnson & Johnson, 68
Johnson Wax, 14
Joint ventures
  case histories of, 9–11
  in Shanghai, 6, 7
  in Zhuhai, 7
Journalism Research Institute of China Social Science Academy, 79
JWT China, 68

Káige TV, 89
Kentucky Fried Chicken, 32
Kissinger, Henry, xv
Kodak, 35, 68, 76, 83
Kodak Photography, xxiii
Konica cameras, 89
Kun Shan, 31
Kuomintang (Nationalist) party, xxiv

Languages, 22
  Gan dialect, 22
  Kejia (Hakka) dialect, 22
  northern dialect, 22
  northern Min dialect, 22
  written, 22–23
  Wu dialect, 22
  Xiang dialect, 22
  Yue dialect (Cantonese), 22
Lao Zi, 89
Lever Brothers, xxvi, 68
Liang Mian Zhen Toothpaste, 43

Liang Xiang, 7
Liberation Daily, 71
Lido Beijing, 68
Light boxes, 77
Light industrial products, 3
Light industry, development of, 1
Li Jingwei, 44–45
Ling, C. P., xxii, xxiii
Lin Zhen Bin (C. P. Ling), xxii
Liquor advertising, control of, 90
Lisu Poles and Swords Festival,
    24
Liuzhou, 35
Lufthansa Airlines, 14, 40, 68, 88
Lux Beauty Soap, xxvi, 83, 88
Luxury spending, 26–27

Magazines, 73–74
Mailing lists, 78
Marketing, application of
    Western techniques to, 31–
    36
Marketing mix, 33–34
Market research, 32
Market segmentation, 31, 32
Market share, role of advertising
    in, 43
Market survey, 32
    for Philips International, 86–
    87
Matsushita Electric Industrial
    Co., 13
Maxam, 43
Maxwell House, 75, 79
May Fourth Movement, xxiv
Mazu Islands, 17
McDonnell Douglas, 68
Media reach surveys
    in Beijing, 79–82
    in Zhejiang Province, 82
Miao New Year Festival, 24
Mid-Autumn Festival, 24
Millington Ltd., xxiii
Ming Dynasty, xvii, xviii

Minhang Economic and
    Technological Development
    Zone, 5
Mini sales exhibitions, 78–79
Mirinda Orange, 42
Mitsubishi, 89
Mobil, 40
Models, use of, 53
Mongolian Nadam Fair, 24

Nanjing, 64
Nanyang Brothers Tobacco
    Company, 31
National Bank of Pakistan, 88
National brand, 13
National character, survey of,
    27–29
National Export Advertising
    Service, xxii
Neon signs, xxii, xxv, 77
Nescafe, 40, 79
Netobimin, 15
Newsletters, xxiii
Newspaper ads, 40, 52
Newspapers
    China Daily, 72–73
    Chinese, xxi
    People's Daily, 71–72
New York Stock Exchange, 39
Nike, 68
Nonalcoholic drink output, 43
Northwest Airlines, 77, 88

O Cedar Wax Cream, 55
Ogilvy & Mather, 36, 68
Omega watch, 41, 53
Open Door Policy, 4–5
Opium War, xviii
Orange Tang, 33, 40, 79
Outch, William, 15
Outdoor advertising, 77–78

Panasonic, 123
Parker, 68
Peasant's Daily, 71
Pension payments to retired
    persons, 25
People's Daily, 71
    advertising rate of, 72
    overseas edition, 72
People's Liberation Army, 71
Pepsi-Cola, 33, 41, 42, 43, 68
Personal selling, 33
Pharmaceuticals, advertisements
    for, 90
Philips International, 68, 75, 76
    market survey for, 86–87
Photography, as advertising tool,
    53
PIA (Pakistan International
    Airlines), 88
Polaroid, 68
Polish Airlines, 88
Political Official Gazette, xxi
Polo Pens, 59
Population, 17–21, 25
Posters, xxii, 40
Private businesses,
    transformation of, to whole
    people enterprises, xxv
Procter & Gamble, 75
Production, absorbing foreign
    techniques of, 1
Product loyalty, xvi
Promotional mix, 33–34
Promotions, 33, 79
Publicity, 33
Public Opinion Institute of
    People's University, 83
Public relations, 39–40, 79

Qi Delin, 40
Qing government, xvii–xviii, xviv

Radio advertising, 74
Radio broadcasting, xxii

Radio and TV publications, 76
Rado Watch, 26
Reference News, 71
Reforms, endorsement of, 4
Reynolds, R. J., Tobacco
    International, Inc., 16, 68
Ricoh, 89
Royal Bank of Canada, 88
Royal Crown, 41, 42
Ruby Cosmetics, 60
Rural families, predicted
    spending for, 28
Rural market, 29
Rural poverty, 29

Saeed Jumma Al Naboodah, 12
Sales promotion, 33, 39–40
    regulation of giveaways, 90
Sample promotions, 40, 79
Sanshui Winery, 45
Sanyo, 41
Schering Corporation, 15
Series advertising, 89
Service centers, 41
7-UP, 41, 42
Shaanxi, 83
Shandong Province, 35
Shanghai, 5, 11, 40, 41, 60, 64,
    68, 83
    adoption of an open door
        policy by, 3
    characteristics of foreign
        investments in, 7–8
    development of foreign trade
        in, 3
    economic and technological
        zones in, 5–6
    economic role of, 2–3
    gross national product of, 9
    industrial output of, 2
    joint ventures in, 6, 7
    opening of port of, xviii
    per-capita income of, 2
    shipyards of, 3

Shanghai Advertising
    Corporation, 32, 64, 67, 78
Shanghai Advertising and
    Decorating Corporation, 64,
    67
Shanghai Advertising Exhibition,
    59
Shanghai Art-designing
    Company, 64
Shanghai Branch Bank of China,
    8
*Shanghai Broadcasting and TV
    Weekly*, 76
Shanghai Caohejing Hi-Tech
    Park, 6
Shanghai Consumer Chemical
    Industrial Development
    Corporation, 14
Shanghai Da Jiang Co., Ltd., 12
Shanghai Federation of Industry
    and Commerce, 39
Shanghai Foreign Trade
    Corporation, 39
Shanghai Industrial Consultants,
    32
Shanghai Industry and
    Commerce Development
    Corporation, 39
Shanghai Johnson, 14
Shanghai No. 1 Department
    Store, 26, 77, 78, 79
Shanghai No. 2 Department
    Store, 27, 78–79
Shanghai No. 2 Pharmaceutical
    Factory, 15
Shanghai People's Radio, 65
Shanghai Soap, xxvi
Shanghai Squibb Pharmaceuticals
    Ltd., 12
Shanghai Telephone, 48
Shanghai Television, 76
Shanghai TV, 65
Shanghai Volkswagen
    Automotive Co., Ltd., 8, 9–
    10, 41, 68
Shanghai Wang Computer
    Development Co., 14–15

Shanghai Watch Factory, 40
Shanghai Xin Yi Wooltex
    Corporation, 11
Shanghai Yaohua Pilkington
    Glass Corporation, 13
Shanxi Province, 12
Shenzhen City Happiness Soft
    Drink Factory, 42
Shenzhen Special Economic
    Zone, 5
Shimonoseki, Treaty of, xviv
Showrooms, 41
Shun Pao, xxi
Sichuan, 83
Siemens, 68
Singapore Airlines, 77
Singer Sewing Machine Corp.,
    Inc., 16
Sino-American Johnson Ltd., 14
Sino-American Shanghai Squibb
    Pharmaceuticals Ltd., 10–11
Sino-American Suzhou Capsugel
    Ltd., 12
Sino-American Tianmei Food
    Co., Ltd., Tianjin, 79
Sino-Sweden Pharmaceutical Co.,
    Ltd., 12
Sino-U.S. Foxboro Co., Ltd., 6
Sin Wan Pao, xxi
Small White Rabbit toothpaste,
    44
Smith, Kennedy & Co., xviii
Smithkline Beckman, 13
Socialist economy, managing a,
    1–2
Society of Journalism, Beijing, 79
Soft drink market, competition
    research in, 41–43
Solar calendar, 23–24
Songjiang County, 11
Sony, 77
Special economic zones, 5–7
Sponsorship, 40, 79
Spring Festival, 24
Standard Chartered Bank, 68
State Council of the People's
    Republic of China for the

Encouragement of Foreign Investment, provisions of, 119–24
Streetcars, xxi
Sun Sun Company, xxii
Suzhou, 11, 31
"Sweetie Spearmint," 57
Swiss Schindler Holdings AG, 11

Tagamet, 13
Taiwan Province, 17
Target market, 31, 32
Telefunken, 77
Television sets, Chinese manufacture of, 83
Temple of Heaven Essential Balm, 36
Textile products, 3
Textile workshops, xvii
Theragran-M, 11
Third World Advertising Congress, 40, 69, 71
Tiananmen Square, xxv
Tianfu Cola, 42–43
Tianjin, 5, 38, 64, 83
Tianjin Daihatsu, 10
Tianjin Economic and Technical Development Area, 5
Tianjin Hebei Pharmaceutical Co., 13
Tibetan New Year Festival, 24
Tien De (God's Virtue) Medical News, xxiii, 1
Toothpaste, 58
Toothpaste market, competition research in, 43–44
Toshiba, 83, 89
Toyota Motor Corporation, 40
Trademark Law of the People's Republic of China, 93–102
Transit advertising, 77
Tsingtao Beer, 35–36
Turner & Co., xviii
TV advertising, 75–76
TV commercials, 90

Unisys, 68
United Airlines, 39, 77
United States, investors from, 8
Utility companies, foreign-owned, 48

Walmsley Ltd., 86
Wang Bingqian, 8
Warner-Lambert, 16
Wartsila, 68
Wen Hui Bao, 71
Westernization, reforms aimed at hastening, xx
Westernization Group, xviv
Western techniques, application of, to marketing, 31–36
Western trademarks, 85
Westinghouse refrigerator, 49
West Lake TV, 35
Wheelock & Co., xviii
Whole people enterprises, transformation of private businesses to, xxv
Window displays, 77–78
Women's Magazine, xxii
Worker's Daily, 71
World Ad Expo, 70
Wuxi, 31

Xiamen, 6
Xi Bi Da Medicated Toothpaste, 44
Xin Min Wan Bao, 71
Xu Bai Yi, 59, 70

Yangchen Wan Bao, 71
Yantai, 5, 35
Yaohua Pilkington Glass Corporation, 8
Yi Torch Festival, 24
Youth Generation, 74
Yung Fang face cream, 26

Zental, 13
Zhao Ziyang, 3
Zhejiang Province, media reach
   survey in, 82
Zhong Hua Toothpaste, 60
Zhong Wan Sin Pao, xxi
Zhuhai, joint ventures in, 7
Zou Erjun, 6

About the Author

Xu Bai Yi was born in Shanghai in December 1911. At the age of 17 he joined United Advertising Advisors. Xu left United in 1923 to join Consolidated National Advertising, one of the four largest advertising agencies in pre-Liberation Shanghai, where he worked first as a copywriter and later as chief copyeditor in the foreign department. He also worked as an editor on the magazine *Advertising & Selling*

In 1941 Xu left Consolidated to set up his own small advertising agency. Working out of his home with a small staff, he had such accounts as Frigidaire, Bayer Aspirin, and Shanghai Worsted Mill. The agency lasted until 1956 when all privately run businesses were reformed into joint state and privately owned companies and later into state-owned companies.

Xu was assigned to the state-controlled Shanghai Advertising Corporation until the start of the Cultural Revolution in 1966. Along with millions of city dwellers, Xu was sent to a farming commune for "re-education." He was permitted to retire in 1972. In November 1979 Xu was called back to advertising in Shanghai as an advisor to the research department of the Shanghai Advertising and Decoration Corporation.

A frequent contributor to *International Advertising* and *China Ad-*

vertising, China's leading trade publications, Xu has also written a number of textbooks on the practices and techniques of advertising. Since 1986 he has been a member of the International Advertising Association—its only representative from the People's Republic.

2847